BORN

TO

DREAM

Inspiring the Dreamer Within to Create a Life of Purpose and Fulfilment

Dr. John Itakpe

BORN TO DREAM

Copyright © 2023 by **John Itakpe**

Contact Me:

johnitakpe@gmail.com.

All scripture quotations are taken with permission from the English Standard Version (ESV) of the Bible unless otherwise indicated.

PRAISES FOR BORN TO DREAM

For over 25 years of my interaction with Dr. John Itakpe I can boldly say his life as a doctor, husband, father, and pastor etc. is proof that indeed dreams come true.

This book will make real to you Eph 3:20 Message Translation. "God can do anything, you know- far more than you could ever imagine or guess or request in your WILDEST DREAMS! He does it not by pushing us around but by working within us, his Spirit deeply and gently within". Never forget to dream more and do more!
-Albert Oduwole, International Conference Speaker, President, Triumphant Nation Everywhere, Canada

I have known PJ for about 3 decades! Having seen firsthand, I can say without a doubt that your dreams will be realized as you imbibe the tenets of this book. It reflects his own personal journey of integrity, persistence, and tenacity in the realization of God-breathed dreams. It's a book worth reading over and over and, over. Selah! - *Dr. Bayo Emmanuel, MBBS, Physician, United Kingdom*

"Born to Dream" is an enraptured probe of the limitless ability we enjoy in Christ in our quest to max out our potentials. Dr. Itakpe beautifully explored this ability using inspiring anecdotes to bring to life our potential to achieve greatness when we dare to dream. *-Dr. Deji Daramola, DSL, MBBS, MBA, MD, CCFP, AHMP, PGDFamM,Author, Family Physician, Expert in Strategic Leadership, Canada*

Born to Dream is a must-read book for everyone that can be more than they are right now. It is for anyone who wants to fulfill destiny by truly manifesting the unhindered power of God. Dr. Itakpe emphasized the dependence of dreams actualization on God, the truth that stands the test of time. *-Pastor Felix Adenusi, Lead Pastor, Gethsemane Sanctuary Baltimore. MD USA.*

Dr. John's book "Born to Dream" exemplifies a life he has consistently lived. He rose from a humble beginning holding on to the God of the dreams he has in his heart. Little wonder where he is today. I recommend this book as a must read to all. *-Dr Rasaq Olaosebikan MD Msc. Pediatrician New Jersey. USA.*

In Born to Dream, Dr John Itakpe has elucidated a clear path to greatness through finding and fulfilling the dreams God has already planted in our hearts. Dr John masterfully explains why we are God's strategic idea and how God is already invested in us and our success and dream fulfillment. This book is a must for everyone who has ever had a dream but not sure how to pursue it and fulfill it. I was challenged to dream again, dream big, dream through oppositions and limitations, and act on the dream with purpose and passion. Our dreams are connected to our destiny.

I have known Dr John Itakpe for more than 2 decades as at the time of this writing. He lives what he teaches. This is your turn. Get a copy of the book Born to Dream and act on the principles. Your dreams will become a reality! *-Dr Chuka Anude, Physician and Lead Pastor, The Soteria Church Baltimore. Maryland USA.*

Dr. John has authored an exceptional book that I believe is a must-read for anyone aspiring to achieve greatness and success. The attainment of greatness and success in life is intricately tied to the pursuit of dreams. Without dreams, life becomes devoid of meaning. Dr. John's book, *Born to Dream*, embodies this concept splendidly.

I wholeheartedly recommend this book to all individuals who yearn to make a positive impact on the world and leave behind a lasting legacy. By harnessing the power of dreams, Dr. John demonstrates how one can truly transform their life's journey into a purposeful and fulfilling endeavor. *-Adeola Atekoja, Author, Connecting the Dots. CEO, Lodeta Media and Publishing, Maryland, USA.*

Table of Contents

DEDICATION

This book is dedicated to my lovely wife, Rosemary Itakpe and to all who would not stop dreaming.

ACKNOWLEDGEMENT

I want to acknowledge the Holy Spirit, who inspired me to write this book and keep dreaming despite all the challenges and battles of life. I also want to recognize God's people who listened and hopefully were encouraged to live the life of a dreamer, knowing fully well that they were born to dream. Finally, I would like to thank my family for their unrelenting support now and always.

FOREWORD

Dr. John Itakpe, my dear friend and brother, has written a fantastic book titled "Born to Dream," that beautifully outlines the inner world and workings of greatness. John is a remarkable personality with whom I have worked closely in the last 30 years and watched him apply the principles he has carefully presented in this book.

John wrote in this inspiring book that "Dreamers rule the world." And this is true. Everyone who has attained greatness in their endeavors began with a dream. God did not create anyone without any seed in them from birth. That seed is the dream God planted in them from birth. So, whether rich or poor, male or female, whatever your status, you are endowed with the capacity to birth the glorious future you are here for. Your dream encapsulates your lot. Therefore, you are not disadvantaged or limited by anything visible or invisible. Your dream is the mental picture of a preferred future. It is captured vividly in your imagination and becomes a source of inspiration and motivation for becoming everything God has predestined for you.

Your ability to dream and paint in your mind's eyes your desired destination in life will commit God and all forces of heaven to support you and see to its accomplishment.

Born To Dream

In Genesis 13:14

And the Lord said unto Abram, after that lot was separated from him, lift now thine eyes, and look from the place where thou art, northward, and southward, and eastward, and westward: For all the land which thou seest, to thee, will I give it, and to thy seed forever.

The scripture above is a beautiful scripture of how Abraham, the father of faith and our progenitor, became the heir of the world (the whole circle of earthly goods, endowment, riches, and advantage) – and he began with a dream to own the world.

It does not matter your station in life, status, race, gender, and current struggles; if you can dream it, you can become it. Joseph had a glorious dream in his teenage years, but they conspired against him because of his dream. So, he went through the pit and prison but eventually became the Prime Minister of the greatest nation of that time.

Friends, you are born to dream. And as long as you keep dreaming and work at it tenaciously, your dream will become your reality, and you'll experience limitless possibilities.

As you read this book, it will help you live to your fullest, bringing joy to God and humanity. So, if this is your desire – to live a purposeful life – then I invite you to follow John through every page of this book, imbibe the lessons shared, and run with the principles he shares therein. There is no doubting your impact in life if you carry out every counsel John shares in this book. So, dear friends, I welcome you to a journey toward fulfilling your life's purpose!

Dr. Escor Jimmy Emmanuel, Physician and Lead Pastor, RCCG Chapel of Testimony, Port Harcourt Nigeria.

CHAPTER ONE

DREAMERS RULE THE WORLD

Your dream is your vision in pictures. It is a graphic presentation of the vision that God unfolds in your mind.

The seed of every greatness is a dream. Dream is what births great accomplishments. Everyone who ever achieved anything in this world had to first dream about it. They first had a graphic presentation of it in their minds There can be no dining with great people without first dreaming it. If you want to seat and dine with kings, you need to learn to dream. It is where the journey begins. It is the law.

Influenced by the *que sera sera* philosophy, which states that what will be will be, many people think that things just happen and that we have no role to play in initiating them or preventing them from happening. This is far from the truth. Those who rule the world are those who dream. But, first, what is dreaming?

When I talk about dreaming, I am talking about the power to envision a desirable future. John Maxwell defines dream this way: "A dream is an inspiring picture of the future that energizes your mind, will and emotions, empowering you to do everything you can to achieve it." Someone once said "A dream is a mental picture of a preferable future." In other words, your dream is your vision in pictures. It is a graphic presentation of the vision that God unfolds in your mind.

God unfolds certain things to you that He wants to do through your life. This is not some random vision of the night kind of dream. It is not merely some fantasy about a future that finds entry into your mind. And it is not that type of; dream that comes as a result of a multitude of busyness. On the contrary, it is a picture that you see, and it is God-given.

The Teacher wrote in Ecclesiastes 5:3 that

For a dream comes with much business, and a fool's voice with many words.

There are instances when we dream because of the activities that transpired throughout the day, but the kinds of dreams we are discussing in this book are God-given. They are revelations from God based on God's purpose for your life. It is more like God unveiling the blueprint of your life to you. Though it may not be a complete revelation, it is enough to drive you throughout your lifetime. How do you identify a God-given dream? It has certain characteristics.

CHARACTERISTICS OF GOD-GIVEN VISION/DREAM

The Dream Glorifies God

Every dream that is given by God points people back to Him. It is woven around God, either directly or indirectly. People should be able to see God in it. Such dreams are about God and reveal Him to the people. The one significant characteristic of every God-inspired dream is that it brings glory to God's name. We can identify such dream by its message or delivery having a clear focus on God. The logic behind this is simple: dreams that come from God will, by default, bear the signature of God all over them.

A God-given dream does not seek to make a name for itself.

The Dream Advances God's Kingdom

A Godly dream should not just be about God, but it should also be about the Kingdom of God. It should not lift up the name of God and at the same time pull down the body of Christ. It should glorify God and everything under His domain. God-inspired dreams are Kingdom drivers. They are given by God, in the first instance, to promote, propagate and establish the Kingdom of God on earth. As

Born To Dream

Jesus said in his prayer teaching, "Thy Kingdom come; Thy will be done on earth as it is in heaven," God seeks that His Kingdom takes a firm footing in our sinful world. So, a God-given dream has no other purpose than the singular purpose of advancing the Kingdom of God.

Unsure if your dream is inspired by God? Check whether it seeks the advancement of the Kingdom of God here on earth. This is a litmus test for your dream – to see if it aligns with God's purpose or not.

The Dream Empowers Others

A Godly dream is about impacting other people. It's the core aspect of the dream. It does not matter the size of that dream; the outcome should be helping others. The dream should help people develop and be better off in life. This characteristic is very important, because God-given dreams are not self-serving. They serve a higher purpose God and the people!

Any dream that revolves around the dreamer only does not satisfy the characteristic of a dream that is given by God.

The Dream is Future-Focused

Our God is a forward-thinking God. Whatever He does, He does with the future in view. The key to a God-given dream is showing others a picture of the future He has planned out for them. The church, including ministry and church organizations, has a duty to continue to move people forward and show them a clear and better future that God desires for them.

This "better future" is not a creation out of the minds of humans. It is the future that God has made, and not a concoction from the minds of people. Because only a God-given dream will truly help a person or group move towards a purposed future that God has planned out for them. That was exactly what happened to Joseph; he enjoyed a great future because God had first revealed to him through dreams about how great his future would be.

5 Now Joseph had a dream, and when he told it to his brothers they hated him even more. 6 He said to them, "Hear this dream that I have dreamed: 7 Behold, we were binding sheaves in the field, and behold, my sheaf arose and stood upright. And behold, your sheaves gathered around it and bowed down to my sheaf."... 9 Then he dreamed another dream and told it to his brothers and said, "Behold, I have dreamed another dream. Behold, the sun, the moon, and eleven stars were bowing down to me." ... 11 And his brothers were jealous of him, but his father kept the saying in mind. Genesis 37:5-11

The Dream Defeats the Devil

When God sets a dream in motion, it is to accomplish the singular purpose of establishing His Kingdom on earth. However, there cannot be a setting up of God's Kingdom without a simultaneous destruction of Satan's Kingdom. The scripture has told us that the purpose of a Godly dream is to destroy the works of the enemy. The bible says that the singular reason Jesus was manifested was for Him to destroy the works of the enemy (1 John 3:8). Our dreams should tear down the kingdom of darkness.

THE DREAM TEST

In the book, *Put your Dream to the Test*, John Maxwell opined that God wants us to have big dreams, because God Himself is a big God. Here is what John Maxwell wrote:

"I believe God wants us to dream, and to dream big, because He's a big God who wants to do big things and He wants to do them through us."

In the book, John Maxwell asked ten critical questions that helps you validate your dream. They are:

1. The Ownership Question: Is my dream really my dream? "Ordinary people can live extraordinary lives when they follow their dreams... Successful people - those who see and seize their dream - love what they do and do what they love."

2. The Clarity Question: Do I clearly see my dream? "Begin by writing a detailed description of your dream. Make your dream measurable."

3. The Reality Question: Am I depending on factors in my control to achieve my dream? "You need to reach far beyond what you're capable of, but at the same time base what you do on your strength and other factors within your control."

4. The Passion Question: Does my dream compel me to follow it?

5. The Pathway Question: Do I have a strategy to reach my dream? "The real difference between a dream and wishful thinking is what you do day to day."

6. The People Question: Have I included the people I need to realize my dream?

7. The Cost Question: Am I willing to pay the price for my dream?

8. The Tenacity Question: Am I moving closer to my dream?

9. The Fulfillment question: Does working toward my dream bring satisfaction?

10. The Significance Question: Does my dream benefit others?

Without a dream today, there will be no future tomorrow. It is today's dream that gives rise to the tomorrow we desperately look forward to. Men that dream, always have something to look forward to and to live for. Dream inspires hope and resilience in the face of opposition and difficulties. Without one, living becomes a mere existence.

The Scripture says in Ephesians 3:20

Now to him who is able to do far more abundantly than all that we ask or think, according to the power at work within us.

Now to Him who is able to [carry out His purpose and] do superabundantly more than all that we dare ask or think [infinitely beyond our greatest prayers, hopes, or dreams], according to His power that is at work within us. (AMP)

Hallelujah! God can cause your wildest dreams to come to pass. It does not matter how wild or out of the ordinary it is, God Almighty can bring it to pass. What is stopping you from dreaming?

From Noah to Abraham and down to the Apostles, there wasn't anyone who didn't catch a glimpse of what God intended to do with their lives. It is the dream (or vision) they had that birthed the greatness that accompanied their names. Tell me one man who was able to change his world without a dream. Tell me one man who was able to change his world without first being a thinker. Successful organizations like Meta (formerly Facebook), Amazon, and Microsoft, are products of dreams. The people behind these organizations have made (and continue to make) significant influences in our lives because they dreamt and dared to pursue their dreams.

You too can rule the world if you can dream. What are you waiting for? Start dreaming today!

CHAPTER TWO

YOU ARE BORN A DREAMER

Our God is a God who dreams and since we are made in His
likeness and image, we should dream too.

A lot takes place during our childhood. These formative years are when our identities take shape, and ideologies become concrete. But it is true also that these are the periods when we begin to visualize the future that we desire. However ridiculous and laughable these dreams might be, childhood is when we first begin to visualize the future that we want to be a part of. I'm sure some of you are probably laughing yourselves out as you reminisce on your childhood dreams right now. It's quite fascinating to know that we might not be born again at the time, yet we had a good idea of what we wanted to become in life. This can only mean that everyone shares an innate ability to dream. God created us with such capacity. You are wired to dream and to dream big.

In Genesis 37, we see the ever-fresh story of Joseph and his siblings. In his dream, Joseph had a glimpse of what he would become in the future. Joseph's dream and his reality at the time share a stark contrast. But this did not deter him from dreaming. The Scripture captures his dream in verse 7:

Behold, we were binding sheaves in the field, and behold, my sheaf arose and stood upright. And behold, your sheaves gathered around it and bowed down to my sheaf."

When his brothers heard the dream, they hated him. Why? They hated him because they understood the meaning of the dream. I'm certain Joseph had no clue what God had revealed to him. Though his brothers hated him because of his dream, joseph didn't stop dreaming. The young lad had the guts to dream again. Don't let anything – your experiences, present reality, people's opinion, oppositions, difficulties, name it – prevent you from dreaming.

The bible records that he dreamt again in verse 9

Then he dreamed another dream and told it to his brothers and said, "Behold, I have dreamed another dream. Behold, the sun, the moon, and eleven stars were bowing down to me."

Several times we stop dreaming because the first dream did not come to pass. Josephs' case was different. Despite the opposition, he still dreamt again. The oppositions were not strong enough to prevent him from dreaming. He didn't let the hatred of the people he loved dash his hope of a better future. So, Joseph dreamt again. He had expectations for his future, even though the prevailing circumstances didn't present the future as promising.

I have noticed that a lot of Christians live each day without any expectations whatsoever. The Scriptures say that *"the expectations of the righteous will not be cut off."* Since they are not expecting anything, they will get nothing. It is that simple! Also, it appears that, in today's society, people's ability to dream diminishes as age catches up on them. This should not be so for you as a Christian. At 85, Caleb still asked for the mountain that the Lord promised to give him (Josh 14:10-12). If Caleb, at eighty-five, still dreamt of the mountain that the Lord promised him, you are inexcusable. Don't allow where you are today to kill your dream of where you should be tomorrow. Yes, I know that things may be tough today, but no one pays to dream. Dreaming is free of charge. You ought to keep envisioning that desirable future no matter the circumstance.

It wouldn't be wrong to say that not dreaming is an affront to God, the Creator of the Universe, who made all things, and is in all things. He first conceived the things He made – light, the heavens and the earth, the sky and the land, the herbs, shrubs and trees, and every living creature including man – and then brought them into existence. Our God is a God who dreams and since we are made in His likeness and image (as revealed in Genesis 1:26), we should dream too.

Born To Dream

In other words, we carry the genes to dream as is found in our Father, God. To think otherwise is to make ineffective the Word of God in Ephesians 3:20 which says,

> *Now to him who is able to do far more abundantly than all that we ask or think, according to the power at work within us.*

This verse says there are two ways we make request to God: what we say and what we think. In most cases, people only practice the first one, which is what we say. Rarely do they remember that their thoughts or imaginations are also a form of prayer. The sad thing is that, most of the time, people ask God for things with their lips while negating the prayers with their thoughts. And the result of this is that they do not get desired responses from God.

The acts of faith and dreaming go hand-in-hand because in both instances we move from the unseen to the seen. When we dream, we dream of things we can't see, or what could be. These dreams are realities we want to take shape sometime in the future. Folks, it takes faith to birth a dream. This is because your dream is always bigger than you. God wants His people to be dreamers. He wants us to dream big dreams for Him. And by doing this, we let God do what only Him can do in our lives.

Your dream will require you to develop character qualities and competence necessary for its fulfillment. Simply put, merely conceiving a dream does not mean that you are mature enough to accomplish it yet. It takes growth, counsel, evaluation, and adjustments along the way. God-given dreams will require you to develop your character, your commitment to Him, and your competence. For instance, if God has called you to be a professional athlete, He will put the dream of being a professional athlete in your heart as a child. That dream needs to be watered, nurtured, cared for, and worked on in order to come to fruition. He puts dreams in us in seed form. Through discipline, commitment, tenacity and skill, we become built with requisite capabilities to bring the dreams to reality.

Let us look at the life of Abraham and learn some steps necessary to fulfilling a God-given dream.

STEPS TO A GOD-GIVEN DREAM

First, let's take a look at what Genesis 15:1-6 says:

1 After these things the word of the LORD came to Abram in a vision: "Fear not, Abram, I am your shield; your reward shall be very great." 2 But Abram said, "O Lord GOD, what will you give me, for I continue childless, and the heir of my house is Eliezer of Damascus?" 3 And Abram said, "Behold, you have given me no offspring, and a member of my household will be my heir." 4 And behold, the word of the LORD came to him: "This man shall not be your heir; your very own son shall be your heir." 5 And he brought him outside and said, "Look toward heaven, and number the stars, if you are able to number them." Then he said to him, "So shall your offspring be." 6 And he believed the LORD, and he counted it to him as righteousness.

1. Seek and Serve God – verse 1

The way to see a God-inspired dream is to seek the Creator Himself. Abraham had just come back from winning a war where he served God with the spoils of the war and paid his tithe. He began asking God some questions about who would become his heir and God answered him. Conceiving a God-given dream starts with seeking and serving God. This can be done in the place of prayer, fasting, studying the bible and even in fellowship with other brethren. A God-given dream does not happen overnight. Its picture becomes clearer over the time as we continue to seek and serve Him. You must understand that we are embedded in Him and all things flows from Him.

Jesus, teaching His disciples in John 15:5, said

Yes, I am the vine; you are the branches. Those who remain in me, and I in them, will produce much fruit. For apart from me you can do nothing. (NLT)

Born To Dream

The Scripture also makes it clear that all good gifts come from God. Our God-inspired dreams are good gifts from God. James affirms this when he wrote in chapter 1 and verse 17 that:

Every good gift and every perfect gift is from above, coming down from the Father of lights, with whom there is no variation or shadow due to change.

2. **It will cause you to Fear** – verse 1

When God gives you a dream, the first emotion that will overwhelm you will most likely be fear. It's quite instructive that the first thing that God tells Abraham is fear not. The enormity or absurdity of the dream may instill fear in you. Thoughts like, how shall these things be? Why am I the one? And things like that could cause one to fear. There are several instances in scriptures where people were told not to fear, for example.

- When He told Moses that He would use him to deliver the Israelites, Moses became afraid (Exodus chapters 3 and 4)
- When the angel told Mary that she would carry the Son of God, he told her "Do not be afraid." (Luke 1)
- When Nehemiah got word that his city was in ruin, he was so upset that he cried, mourned and prayed, and then waited

until God opened the door for him to speak to the king. He was also afraid.

Anytime God gives you a dream, you may be frightened. This is understandable considering the fact that God-given dreams are always God-sized. But you have to remember that fear is a spirit, and it is not given by God. So cast it out by believing God and building your faith in the word of God. Sometimes it may be the fear of men, and you'll have to decide if the fear of man or obeying God is more important to you.

3. **A God-given dream is always more than you** – verse 2. (What will thou give me?)

If your dream is from God, it will be bigger, and larger than you. God's dream transcends what you can consume for yourself and family. Abraham was concerned about what God will give him; God was concerned about what he will give to humanity through Abraham. Abraham asked God "What will Thou give me?" Each time our focus is on ourselves, we tend to miss out on what God wants to do. He always wants to use us to be a blessing to others. Am I saying that you will not be blessed through that dream? Definitely, no! The dream will flow from you like a stream. You will drink from it, but it will ultimately flow down to others.

Also, a dream that you can accomplish by yourself is not a God-given dream. If your dream is God-given, you will not be able to accomplish it on your own. You will need God's miraculous intervention to achieve it. God is a believer in community. He is in relationship constantly with Jesus and the Holy Spirit. He could not have accomplished what He did without them. You need others to help your dream come to fruition. They will add to it, speak life into it, pray for it, keep you accountable to it, and make it better than it could have been if you tried to do it alone.

You must also remember that you should never leave the God of the dream to run after the people of the dream. The people are important. As a matter of fact, they're very important. But they are only relevant if you are still holding on to the God of the dream. If you pursue people one of two things will occur:

- People will steal the dream from you.
- People will take you away from God, leaving you to depend on self and no longer on God.

4. A God-given dream will cause you to ask questions – verse 2-3

Anyone who is starting to dream needs to take some time to figure out what the next steps are in the process. The enormity of the task will elicit some questions in your heart. But do not be afraid to ask them. This will help you gain a better perspective of the dream and about what to do, and whether you are headed in the right direction or not. Here are some biblical examples:

- Mary asked: How shall this be, seeing I know not a man? (Luke 1:34)
- Moses asked several questions in Exodus 3
  - Who am I? Exodus 3:11:

    But Moses said to God, "Who am I that I should go to Pharaoh and bring the children of Israel out of Egypt?"
  - What is your name? Exodus 3:13

    Then Moses said to God, "If I come to the people of Israel and say to them, 'The God of your fathers has sent me to you,' and they ask me, 'What is his name?' what shall I say to them?"
  - Exodus 4:1

    Then Moses answered, "But behold, they will not believe me or listen to my voice, for they will say, 'The LORD did not appear to you.'"
  - Exodus 4:10

    But Moses said to the LORD, "Oh, my Lord, I am not eloquent, either in the past or since you have spoken to your servant, but I am slow of speech and of tongue."

5. **A God-given dream is always an original** – verse 4. "...Thine own bowel"

Born To Dream

God is too big to duplicate dreams. His dream for you is always an original. Everyone that carries a God-given dream shares striking similarities to a pregnant woman. Every pregnancy and child of a woman holds a significant distinctiveness, and both the experience and the child are very personal and unique. When she gives birth to the child, something leaves her that is hers.

So, it is important to know that God wants you to birth a dream too. Rather than seek God, people duplicate dreams that have been conceived and birthed by someone else. Seek God first and He will drop that specific dream that He wants you to fulfill in your heart – the very reason he created you. If you can conceive it, then it's an original for you to pursue and birth. Do you remember the story of the woman that stole the child of another woman in 1 Kings 3:16-28? You do not need to steal some other persons' dream. God can give you your dream – though it may share semblance with the other persons' dream, it still is an authentic dream to you.

However lofty the idea of conceiving and birthing a dream is, that's not the end. Dreams must be sustained. To sustain and keep a dream alive, sacrifice is a must. You must be willing to sacrifice something or everything to see that dream come to pass.

6. **A God-inspired dream is God-sized**

Born To Dream

God gives you the latitude to dream big. There is no God-given dream that is too big for God to fulfill. Oftentimes, we view God from the limitations we had during our childhood experiences with our parents, or even by our limitations as parents (if married). For example, when our children make demands beyond what we have capacity for, the default response would be a "no." But let me remind you that our God is not like that. As a matter of fact, God surpasses those dreams and aspirations in our hearts. God brought Abraham abroad and asked him to look. H did not ask him to look out of the window but brought him forth to a large place where no matter how he looked, he would keep seeing.

7. **It's about the kingdom of God** – verse 5 "...*look toward heaven*"

Have you asked yourself the important question: "Where is God in this dream? Remember, if God gave you the dream, it should bring benefits to the Kingdom of God. Whose kingdom are you trying to build? Will this dream make you look good to your peers, family, or friends? Or are you willing to pursue the dream because, in the end, you know that God will get the glory in it? You need to know the difference.

The Bible says it is in our weakness that God's strength is made perfect. Are you relying on your own strength, believing you can do this on your own, or do you realize it's going to be a miracle done by God if this dream becomes a reality?

In benefitting the kingdom of God, it must touch the lives of the people. This is ultimately what a God-given dream should do. There is no larger dream or vision than the one God dreamed for us, by sending His Son Jesus as a ransom to redeem us back to Him. It is only through Him that we have our dignity affirmed.

We are righteous only through Him. We are worthy because of the stripes of Jesus. That is how God brought us into His kingdom.

8. **Believe Your Dream**.

The real evidence that you believe the dream is in your pursuit of it. Abraham believed God, and he lived the rest of the days pursuing the dream that God gave him. About Abraham, the scripture says

> *By faith Abraham, when he was tested, offered up Isaac, and he who had received the promises was in the act of offering up his only son, 18 of whom it was said, "Through Isaac shall your offspring be named." 19 He considered that God was able even to raise him from the dead, from which, figuratively speaking, he did receive him back.* Hebrews 11:17-19

Can you believe God enough to pursue and sacrifice all that is necessary to fulfill that God-inspired dream of yours?

Born To Dream

When I speak with people who have newly migrated to the United States, I tell them that they can become whatsoever they dream to become here. It does not matter where you are coming from. You have the latitude here to dream and become it by the grace of God. When you believe a thing, it is seen in what you say.

In verse 5, the Bible says, *"tell the stars."* That clause connotes a vocalization of the numbering of the stars. Your confession is the first step to living your dream. The fastest way the enemy steals your dream is by keeping you quiet.

In the story of Joseph, I know a lot of people would say that if Joseph had not told his brothers and parents about his dream, he would not have had all the troubles he had. But I beg to differ. If he had not spoken out about his dream, it might have just remained within him. His proclamation propelled the heavens to move into action for his good. What are you saying about those dreams of yours?

CHAPTER THREE

DARE TO DREAM BIG

There is something you have that blossoms when it is in the hands of God. Everyone has been given something by God that gives you an advantage.

In Genesis chapter 1, we see the story of the creation of the earth, how from nothing and chaos, God created the earth in 6 days. He looked inwards and spoke what he saw instead of what he saw on the outside. Now more than 6000 years afterwards, we are still living on this earth. It is estimated that man occupies only about 10% of the earth's surface. It is also thought that more than seventy percent of the earth's surface is water. When we also consider that we have a vast expanse of land used for farming, you can only imagine how big God's dream of the earth alone is, not to talk of the galaxies.

As a parent, my desire is that my children will be greater than I am (And I know they will be). I believe this is the desire of every godly parent. God is our Father, and He created us in His likeness and image. So, if he had such a big dream in creating the world, then you, too, should dream big. Our God is a big God and will make sure that our dreams come to pass. God does not think small. God will always do more than we desire or ask of Him. The beautiful thing about our God is the fact that He is not just sending us good words, but also watches over His Word to perform it.

For instance, if Jeff Bezos tells me, "Hey, John, pick any item of your choice on Amazon. The bill is on me." First, the thought of Jeff not having enough money to pay for it won't cross my mind. Second, I would most likely pick the most expensive thing whether I want it or not – maybe I would sell it off later to get the money if I really do not want it. But the thought that "Will Jeff be able to pay for it" will not be an issue. He does not just have enough money to pay for anything I desire from Amazon, but, as a matter of fact, he is the owner of Amazon itself.

Yet in all the greatness of Jeff, he is in the tiniest of fraction comparable to our God. The God we serve is bigger than a trillion Jeff Bezos multiplied one billion times. There is no basis for comparison at all. I want us to be rest assured that there is no dream we will have that will be too big for our God to fulfill.

Searching through scriptures, there are more than enough examples showing us the ability of God.

1. **God is able to keep us from sin**

Now to him who is able to keep you from stumbling and to present you blameless before the presence of his glory with great joy. – Jude 24

Our God has the power to keep us from falling into sin. He saved you not to let you down. Having once walked on this earth, he knows what it is to be tempted (Hebrews 2:18) and therefore, He is able to keep you from falling into sin.

2. God is able to save us completely

Consequently, he is able to save to the uttermost those who draw near to God through him, since he always lives to make intercession for them. – Hebrews 7:25

Our God is not just able to save us from sinning here on earth, He is able to also save us on the last day, when we will be with Him forever.

3. He Is Able to Heal Our Diseases

After raising Jairus' daughter from death, Jesus met two blind men right after He emerged from the house. The two men cried out, "Have mercy on us, Son of David!" Jesus asked them, "Do you believe that I am able to do this?" (Matthew 9:27-28) and they answered, "Yes, Lord," Jesus then touched their eyes and healed them. Jesus is able to heal you from every and any infirmity if you believe that He is able to do so.

Born To Dream

4. God is Able to Supply Our Needs

And God is able to make all grace abound to you, so that having all sufficiency in all things at all times, you may abound in every good work. 2 Corinthians 9:8

God is able to make all gracious gifts come to you in abundance. It does not matter what your needs are, God will supply your needs and give you more than enough to be a blessing to others.

5. God is able to Deliver from Physical Death

When Shadrach, Meshach and Abednego were confronted with death penalty if they refused to bow and worship the golden image made by King Nebuchadnezzar, in Daniel 3:16-18, they "answered and said to the king, O Nebuchadnezzar, we are not careful to answer thee in this matter." Here's what the Scripture says:

17 If this be so, our God whom we serve is able to deliver us from the burning fiery furnace, and he will deliver us out of your hand, O king. 18 But if not, be it known to you, O king, that we will not serve your gods or worship the golden image that you have set up."

What a show of boldness and confidence from these three Hebrew friends! They were convinced that God will deliver them, but if for any reason He chooses not to, they would still not bow to the king's golden image. God indeed delivered them from the furnace and saved their lives.

6. God is able to Exceed our Expectations

Now to him who is able to do far more abundantly than all that we ask or think, according to the power at work within us. Ephesians 3:20

I am always excited when I recite this passage of Scripture. Our God is not just able to answer our prayers, but He is also able to cause our wildest dreams to come true. Pause for a moment and think about this text. It says that God gives thought to the things you ask and the things you think about. It is a sad reality that our asking, many times, does not align with our thinking or imaginations. This is one of the reasons, I believe, our prayers go unanswered. We ask God for something but in our thoughts, we keep thinking that it will not come to pass. You must realize that your thoughts are as powerful as your speech. Think in line with God's Word for your prayers.

7. God is Able to Keep Whatsoever is Committed to Him

Which is why I suffer as I do. But I am not ashamed, for I know whom I have believed, and I am convinced that he is able to guard until that day what has been entrusted to me. – 2 Timothy 1:12

Our God is able to keep anything we commit to him. He is trustworthy and you can always count on Him. Also, God will never abandon you. You can trust him to stand with you through thick and thin, until the end.

Some believers might think that when Jesus comes, they might miss the rapture. But I want you to be assured that God will keep you till the end. He saved you not to leave you here.

8. God is a Performer

Fully convinced that God was able to do what he had promised. – Romans 4:21

Our God does not just talk. He is also a performer. God is not like those people who are big in words but small in deeds. When our God says a thing on the other hand, he does not just have the capability to do it, He does it. Anything God says will come to pass. If that thing does not exist, it will be created. Our God is able to perform whatsoever he says. What has God told you that seems to be delaying, trust God and hold on to His word, He will perform it. He spoke to Abraham about giving him a child. It appeared as though, God's words will not come to pass with the passage of time, but God showed up. Time never starts counting until God shows up. Remember, God lives outside time, so when God shows up is really

Born To Dream

when time starts counting. Hold on to God's word for it will never fail.

NECESSITIES FOR DREAMING BIG

1 On one occasion, while the crowd was pressing in on him to hear the word of God, he was standing by the lake of Gennesaret, 2 and he saw two boats by the lake, but the fishermen had gone out of them and were washing their nets. 3 Getting into one of the boats, which was Simon's, he asked him to put out a little from the land. And he sat down and taught the people from the boat. 4 And when he had finished speaking, he said to Simon, "Put out into the deep and let down your nets for a catch." 5 And Simon answered, "Master, we toiled all night and took nothing! But at your word I will let down the nets." 6 And when they had done this, they enclosed a large number of fish, and their nets were breaking. 7 They signaled to their partners in the other boat to come and help them. And they came and filled both the boats, so that they began to sink. – Luke 5:1-7

For the purpose of this teaching, I want you to look at the vast amount of water (ocean) as the possible zone that they can fish in. In this instance, the bible says they were at the bank of the waters.

1. Hear the Word of God

This Book of the Law shall not depart from your mouth, but you shall meditate on it day and night, so that you may be careful to do according to all that is written in it. For then you will make

your way prosperous, and then you will have good success. –
Joshua 1:8

*1 I will take my stand at my watchpost and station myself on the
tower, and look out to see what he will say to me, and what I will
answer concerning my complaint. 2 And the LORD answered me:
"Write the vision; make it plain on tablets, so he may run who
reads it.* – Habakkuk 2:1-2

The Lord gave Peter a word to launch into the deep. The word of
God created the avenue for Peter to dream again. Your obedience to
the word brings into reality the dream that has been cast in your
heart. This is how a God-given dream works. It was through the
word that the world was created.

2. Enter your Boat

That is the vehicle that they had to go into the waters. What is that
thing that has been given to you to make a difference? For Joseph, it
was the interpretation of dreams. For David, it was his musical skills
and exceptional love for and trust in God; for Gideon, it was his
courage and leadership.

There is something you have, that blossoms when it is in the hands
of God. Every one of us has been given something by God that gives
us an advantage. Some may be conspicuous, while some others may

not. But every one of us has an edge that God expects us to leverage for our growth and launching.

This vehicle takes you out, a little at a time. But when you dream again, it launches you further. As you discover that thing that gives you an edge and continue to leverage it, it moves you deeper into becoming that man and woman of your dreams. You dream from the known to the unknown. Joseph knew his father and siblings will bow to him but the situation and time was not known to him.

3. Launch out into the Deep

Folks, you've got to dream big. Once again, there is a big similarity between faith and dreams. However, both entail a process of seeing the unseen and bringing it into reality. You need to believe God to launch out into the deep. To launch out into the deep means you are ready to risk it based on God and His promises. Jesus did not instruct Peter to launch out at the banks of the river but to launch out into the deep. Look at the vastness of the water and go as far as you can inwards and then cast the net. When God spoke with Abraham in Genesis 15, he told him to look towards heaven and 'tell the stars.' How big can you dream? God is interested in stretching your imagination. Once you are stretched by a God-given vision, you never snap back into your original shape again!

To 'Launch out' could mean:

- Setting goals and establishing a plan to reach them.
- Staying tuned to God's leadings.
- Confronting old fears.
- Devoting your life to something greater than yourself.
- Having a "Thou art with me" attitude!

4. Let down your Nets

A man that dreams and does not let down his net is only wishing. Obedience is the crucible through which dreams are formed and forged. You might have been carrying that dream for so long, now is the time to let go and let God. God instructed Peter to let down his nets, and Peter did just that. Peter's obedience was pivotal in his journey of following Christ and leading the early Church. In the same way that Peter and the other fishermen were amazed at the huge catch of fish they had, obedience to God leads us into a spacious place of God's endless goodness and blessings.

CHAPTER FOUR

BREAKING LIMITATIONS. DOING THE UNIMAGINABLE

You are created and designed to do the unimaginable and you have the capacity to break every barrier on your path to realizing your God-given dreams.

Generations after generations, certain individuals have stood up to show the world that limitations are nothing but walls built by people around their minds. One of such people are the Wright Brothers – Wilbur and Orville Wright. On December 17, 1903, the Wright brothers made a giant leap in aerodynamics, creating one of the first airplanes that could be powered, sustained and controlled. But a few years before this, in 1899, the commissioner of the US patents office, Charles Duell, tendered his resignation letter. In his resignation letter, Duell wrote that *"We have reached the end. Everything that can be invented has been invented."* But in less than five years, Wright Brothers invented something that changed the aviation industry forever.

Born To Dream

People like Charles Duell exist today. They mount walls of impossibilities in their minds and project these walls at people who are doing something worthwhile with their lives, trying to change the world. You must not listen to them, or give their words a place in your mind. They throw jabs at you, making a mockery of what you're doing. But you must not let them discourage you or cower you into silence.

Nehemiah, in his bid to rebuild the walls of Jerusalem, faced stiff opposition from Sanballat, Tobiah and Geshem. These men were grieved that someone sought the welfare of Jerusalem and its people. When the work of rebuilding Jerusalem's wall began, the men mocked Nehemiah and his team.

> *And I told them of the hand of my God that had been upon me for good, and also of the words that the king had spoken to me. And they said, "Let us rise up and build." So they strengthened their hands for the good work. 19 But when Sanballat the Horonite and Tobiah the Ammonite servant and Geshem the Arab heard of it, they jeered at us and despised us and said, "What is this thing that you are doing? Are you rebelling against the king?" 20 Then I replied to them, "The God of heaven will make us prosper, and we his servants will arise and build, but you have no portion or right or claim in Jerusalem."* Nehemiah 2:18-20

Born To Dream

But Nehemiah and the people did not cease from the divine dream that God had given to Nehemiah. They continued to work in the midst of oppositions. Your God-inspired dream will attract mockers and naysayers like Sanballat, Tobiah, and Geshem. They will say all kinds of unkind words to you. These people will show you a million reasons why your dream is impossible. But you must stick to the God who gave you the dream in the first place, believe the dream and pursue its realization.

The presence of men like Sanballat in your life is a testament that you're doing something worthwhile. Like the popular saying, no one throws stones at a tree that has no fruits on it. So, when they throw their stones at you, build castle with it. When they serve you lemons, make lemonade out of them. The thing is, don't stop what you're doing. Don't quit on your dream. Quitting must never be an option for you. Instead, use their mockery and opposition to propel your dreams to fruition.

Nehemiah was a man of dogged faith. He was clear about what God had told him. And he's not going to let anything stop him from following God to where He was leading him. The vision to see the glory of Jerusalem restored was enough motivation to keep him going. Nehemiah's venture to rebuild the wall would become a story about doing the unimaginable, because he led the people to finish the rebuilding of Jerusalem's wall in record fifty-two days.

So the wall was finished on the twenty-fifth day of the month Elul,
in fifty-two days. 16 *And when all our enemies heard of it, all the*
nations around us were afraid and fell greatly in their own
esteem, for they perceived that this work had been accomplished
with the help of our God. Nehemiah 6:15-16

If you don't cave into the scorn of men like Sanballat, you, too, like
Nehemiah, will realize your dream. But you must brace yourself up
for oppositions. It is not a matter of if; it is a matter of when. So, don't
pray or wish it away. The presence of mockers and oppositions on
your journey to fulfilling your dream serves a greater purpose if you
can see it. How else will your story be worth telling if you do not face
opposition? How else will your arms be strengthened if you don't
have to fight off dream schemers? How else will you be able to make
lemonade if they don't throw their lemons at you? So, these people,
though with wrong intent, are pivotal to the fulfillment of your
dreams.

People like Sanballat will be there at every stage of your dream. They
will be there at the beginning, in the middle, upon completion, and
during the years of sustaining the vision. Their presence at every
juncture serves to prepare you for the next phase of your dream.
Therefore, don't relent and fold your arms saying, it is over. It is not
over until it is over. Remember that your dream serves the Kingdom
purpose, so it is commonplace for you to face oppositions. The devil

does not want the Kingdom of God to advance. He knows your dream is one avenue by which God wants to expand His rule and reign on earth. That is why he does not relent. Sanballat and his team of mockers were there at every juncture of the rebuilding of Jerusalem's wall

Now when Sanballat heard that we were building the wall, he was angry and greatly enraged, and he jeered at the Jews. 2 And he said in the presence of his brothers and of the army of Samaria, "What are these feeble Jews doing? Will they restore it for themselves? Will they sacrifice? Will they finish up in a day? Will they revive the stones out of the heaps of rubbish, and burned ones at that?" 3 Tobiah the Ammonite was beside him, and he said, "Yes, what they are building—if a fox goes up on it he will break down their stone wall!" Nehemiah 4:1-3

You see, there is no room for thinking that once you've overcome a limitation, another will not come. Limitations always come at every phase of the growth of your dream, from conception to delivery, and nurturing. Their forms may be different, but limitation will always present itself to stop you from advancing. Limitations take different forms. It is important to discuss these forms, and acquaint yourself with strategies to overcoming them.

PHYSICAL LIMITATIONS

Born To Dream

Physical limitations are often the most observable limitations we encounter. The reason is simple: it is physical. This form of limitations comes as physical defects, institutional barriers, and human interference as discussed above. Are you limited by physical defects, and you have resigned from living a fulfilling life? I want to let you know that your physical limitation is not insurmountable. Someone said that "The only thing worse than being blind is having sight but no vision." That person is Helen Keller.

Helen Keller at nineteen months lost her hearing and sight to an illness and not long after, her speech development was affected. But Keller would become the first deaf and blind woman to graduate from college in the United States of America. Additionally, Helen Keller wrote over five hundred essays and speeches, and several books – one of which is the *Story of My Life*. There are countless examples of people who have shown that physical limitations are not enough to keep you from dreaming. You'll learn about these people in Chapter eleven.

Also, there are institutional limitations. These are such limitations that are systemic in nature, making it practically impossible for people's dream to thrive. One such example is the experience of black people during America's dark ages of slavery and post-slavery black segregation. In such instances where it was difficult to dream, there were still men and women who rose above these limitations to actualize their dreams.

MENTAL LIMITATIONS

Mental limitations are more or less a siege we have erected around our minds. These might have resulted from past experiences, or simply laziness of the mind to refuse a certain present predicament or condition. In some nations, it is commonplace to see able-bodied men and women who have resorted to begging for alms for survival. In most cases, these people have preconditioned their minds for this kind of life, refusing all forms of help or intervention to live a more promising life.

The children of Israel, when they had left Egypt after hundreds of years of slavery, were still strongly enslaved in their minds. Many times, along their journey to the Promised Land, they wished Moses had left them in Egypt. Physical freedom does not automatically translate to mental freedom. It took them another forty years in the desert to undo the slavery shackles that bound their minds. God had to make sure that a certain generation that left Egypt perished in the desert in order to purge them of the mental enslavement.

and the people of Israel said to them, "Would that we had died by the hand of the LORD in the land of Egypt, when we sat by the meat pots and ate bread to the full, for you have brought us out into this wilderness to kill this whole assembly with hunger." Exodus 16:3

1 Then all the congregation raised a loud cry, and the people wept that night. 2 And all the people of Israel grumbled against Moses and Aaron. The whole congregation said to them, "Would that we had died in the land of Egypt! Or would that we had died in this wilderness! 3 Why is the LORD bringing us into this land, to fall by the sword? Our wives and our little ones will become a prey. Would it not be better for us to go back to Egypt?" 4 And they said to one another, "Let us choose a leader and go back to Egypt." Numbers 14:1-4

For the people of Israel walked forty years in the wilderness, until all the nation, the men of war who came out of Egypt, perished, because they did not obey the voice of the LORD; the LORD swore to them that he would not let them see the land that the LORD had sworn to their fathers to give to us, a land flowing with milk and honey. Joshua 5:6

Though the children of Israel were free from the bondage of Egypt, their minds remained chained to their slave masters and Egypt. You might have passed a difficult phase in your life, but you might still be controlled by those experiences you had while going through that phase. Therefore, you think, act, make decisions and live based on the realities of your past. This way, dreaming or advancing in your dream becomes a difficult issue. Many people live presently in their past. They make decisions and see the world from the lenses of their past experiences. To make reasonable advancement, this barrier must be broken.

SPIRITUAL LIMITATIONS

In the previous chapters, I have established that a God-given dream must advance God's Kingdom here on earth. By implication, the hordes of hell are set to attack this dream and stop it from propagating God's purpose on earth. So, the devil erects barriers to frustrate the realization of the dream God gives us. And we must restrict his assault vehemently. Paul gave us the premise for this form of limitations more clearly when he said that

12 For we do not wrestle against flesh and blood, but against the rulers, against the authorities, against the cosmic powers over this present darkness, against the spiritual forces of evil in the heavenly places. 13 Therefore take up the whole armor of God, that you may be able to withstand in the evil day, and having done all, to stand firm. Ephesians 6:12-13 (NIV)

Born To Dream

You must remind yourselves daily that the ultimate barrier you have to pull down every now and then is the one that your adversary, the devil, sets along your path to fulfilling your dream. You have a divine duty to withstand Satan's onslaught. Paul states categorically that our fight is not with flesh and blood – though it may appear like these are our main opponents. On the contrary, Paul said that the fight is against the rulers, the authorities, the cosmic powers over this present darkness, and the spiritual forces of evil in the heavenly places.

And that is why the weapons of your warfare to pulling down these spiritual barriers must stem from a higher spiritual power – in this case, it is God. Paul again shows us that our weapon of pulling down every spiritual barrier set up against our dreams is through the divine powers of God.

> *3 For though we walk in the flesh, we are not waging war according to the flesh. 4 For the weapons of our warfare are not of the flesh but have divine power to destroy strongholds. 5 We destroy arguments and every lofty opinion raised against the knowledge of God, and take every thought captive to obey Christ, 6 being ready to punish every disobedience, when your obedience is complete.* 2 Corinthians 10:3-6

Beloved, your journey to birthing and fulfilling your God-inspired dreams is a warfare journey. So, you must brace yourself to fight with the power of Christ. And the good news is that this battle was won before it even started. Christ won this victory for you over two thousand years ago at the cross of Calvary. Your duty, therefore, is to enter the war room as a victor, riding upon the victory of our Lord and Savior Jesus Christ.

MAXIMIZING WHO YOU ARE IN CHRIST

Knowing who you are will determine whether or not you will do the unimaginable things that heaven has written concerning you from the beginning of time. You are not a product of accident, regardless of the story surrounding your conception. You are not some ordinary guys on the street. You are not the difficult experiences that have battered you over the years. You are not what the world says you are. You are not an after-thought. And you're definitely not a mistake. So, who are you?

The Word of God has some exciting things to say about who we are. Let's take a look.

You are like Christ

Look at what is before your eyes. If anyone is confident that he is Christ's, let him remind himself that just as he is Christ's, so also are we. 2 Corinthians 10:7

You are blessed by God

Blessed be the God and Father of our Lord Jesus Christ, who has blessed us in Christ with every spiritual blessing in the heavenly places. Ephesians 1:3

You are chosen, loved, and adopted for God's praise and glory

...even as he chose us in him before the foundation of the world, that we should be holy and blameless before him. In love 5 he predestined us for adoption to himself as sons through Jesus Christ, according to the purpose of his will, 6 to the praise of his glorious grace, with which he has blessed us in the Beloved. Ephesians 1:4-6

You are redeemed and forgiven

In him we have redemption through his blood, the forgiveness of our trespasses, according to the riches of his grace, Ephesians 1:7

You have an Inheritance in Christ

In him we have obtained an inheritance, having been predestined according to the purpose of him who works all things according to the counsel of his will. Ephesians 1:11

You have the Holy Spirit

13 In him you also, when you heard the word of truth, the gospel of your salvation, and believed in him, were sealed with the promised Holy Spirit, 14 who is the guarantee of our inheritance until we acquire possession of it, to the praise of his glory. Ephesians 1:13-14

You are alive in Christ Jesus

But God, being rich in mercy, because of the great love with which he loved us, 5 even when we were dead in our trespasses, made us alive together with Christ—by grace you have been saved— 6 and raised us up with him and seated us with him in the heavenly places in Christ Jesus, 7 so that in the coming ages he might show the immeasurable riches of his grace in kindness toward us in Christ Jesus. Ephesians 2:4-7

You are God's strategic idea

For we are his workmanship, created in Christ Jesus for good works, which God prepared beforehand, that we should walk in them. Ephesians 2:10

You are a royalty, chosen and holy

But you are a chosen race, a royal priesthood, a holy nation, a people for his own possession, that you may proclaim the excellencies of him who called you out of darkness into his marvelous light. 1 Peter 2:9

You are a masterpiece created with Divine purpose

13 For you formed my inward parts; you knitted me together in my mother's womb. 14 I praise you, for I am fearfully and wonderfully made. Wonderful are your works; my soul knows it very well. 15 My frame was not hidden from you, when I was being made in secret, intricately woven in the depths of the earth. 16 Your eyes saw my unformed substance; in your book were written, every one of them, the days that were formed for me, when as yet there was none of them. Psalm 139:13-16

You have everything you need

3 His divine power has granted to us all things that pertain to life and godliness, through the knowledge of him who called us to his own glory and excellence, 4 by which he has granted to us his precious and very great promises, so that through them you may become partakers of the divine nature, having escaped from the corruption that is in the world because of sinful desire. 2 Peter 1:34

You are from God and have overcome the world

Little children, you are from God and have overcome them, for he who is in you is greater than he who is in the world. 1 John 4:4

The list is endless. You are no ordinary person. You have immense capabilities to break every limitation on your way, and do the unimaginable through the power of God at work in you. Don't give room to the naysayers to quench the fire of your dream. Don't give mockers an inch in your mind. Instead, let the floodlight of God's Word find a residence in your heart, animating your thoughts, actions, and decisions. You are created and designed to do the unimaginable and you have the capacity to break every barrier on your path to realizing your God-given dreams.

CHAPTER FIVE

ENCOURAGE YOURSELF TO LIVE YOUR DREAM

You should never give up on your dream. Keep at it. Try again and again, and someday, you will get there.

The story of Diana Nyad readily came to mind when I was writing this chapter. Diana, at the age of sixty-four, swam from Cuba to Florida without the aid of a shark cage. She swam 111 miles in 53 hours from Havana to Key West on September 2, 2013. The Guinness Book of Records has it that she had previously attempted it 4 times. Folks, it does not matter, how many times you fail, you have to encourage yourself to live your dream.

You should never give up on your dream. Keep at it. Try again and again, and someday, you will get there. Diana Nyad was 64 years old when she achieved this great feat after four failed attempts. It shows that you are never too old to take a shot at your dream. Some United States immigrants sometimes feel they are too old to start a new career or reinvent themselves. That's a big lie from the devil. Your age should not be a barrier to fulfilling your dream. If your heart says yes, and your head says no, please follow your heart, because you truly can. At the age of eighty-five, Caleb was unrelenting in his quest to take the mountain that God promised him.

What is that dream that keeps you up at night? You need to encourage yourself to live that dream in spite of all the challenges you are encountering. To encourage means to inspire with courage. In other words, in spite of the opposition you need to persuade yourself to move on. Oppositions are inevitable on this journey. So, you must brace yourself to face and overcome every form of oppositions. But how do you know what you're facing is an opposition? There are signs you will see that tells you you're in the face of oppositions.

CARDINAL SIGNS OF OPPOSITION YOU WILL SEE ON YOUR QUEST TO FULFILLING YOUR DREAM

People hate you for no just cause

Joseph's brothers hated him for no good reason. They didn't like him, not necessarily for what he did, but also for what he did not do. There are times when you cannot place your hands on what you did or did not do that warranted the hatred you receive. Your haters must have hung around you long enough to hear words from your mouth that they are simply not comfortable with. To be clear, these are not bad desires. On the contrary, they are words that convey who you are and where you're going to in life. Such words are our defaults, and they're spoken consciously or unconsciously. For example, if you stay around me long enough, you will know what I stand for and where I am going.

The Scripture says in Genesis 37:4-11,

> *But when his brothers saw that their father loved him more than all his brothers, they hated him and could not speak peacefully to him. 5 Now Joseph had a dream, and when he told it to his brothers they hated him even more. 6 He said to them, "Hear this dream that I have dreamed: 7 Behold, we were binding sheaves in the field, and behold, my sheaf arose and stood upright. And behold, your sheaves gathered around it and bowed down to my sheaf." 8 His brothers said to him, "Are you indeed to reign over us? Or are you indeed to rule over us?" So they hated him even more for his dreams and for his words. 9 Then he dreamed another dream and told it to his brothers and said, "Behold, I have dreamed another dream. Behold, the sun, the moon, and eleven stars were bowing down to me." 10 But when he told it to his father and to his brothers, his father rebuked him and said to him, "What is this dream that you have dreamed? Shall I and your mother and your brothers indeed come to bow ourselves to the ground before you?" 11 And his brothers were jealous of him, but his father kept the saying in mind.*

I can just imagine what went on at Jacob's home during this time. Each time Joseph opened his mouth to say a word, everyone probably shouted back at him to keep quiet. And Joseph would say, "What did I just say that is making them mad at me." Every other person could express themselves but not Joseph. For Joseph, peace among his brothers was a basic luxury he never had.

People conspire against you

Hate may just progress to conspiracy. When hate matures to conspiracy, people will begin to say you did things that you never did. The reason is nor fat-fetched: they cannot stand your guts and everything you represent. Joseph's brothers conspired against him, and sold him to the Ishmaelite merchants who, in turn, sold him to Potiphar in Egypt.

Envy from people

Envy is a powerful emotion. And it could be destructive. This emotion has been present in human nature since The Fall at the Garden of Eden. Cain and Abel's story is a prime example of how destructive envy could be. Envy is a feeling of discontent or resentment that arises when someone else has something that you want or desire. From Cain and Abel's story, the Bible shows envy as a destructive force that can consume a person's heart and mind, and influence their actions negatively. In Genesis chapter 4, Cain's envy towards his brother, Abel, led to violence and death. It was the first recorded murder in human history according to the Bible. Cain's emotion of envy did not only destroy Abel's life, but also resulted in Cain's punishment and expulsion. Envious reactions towards you are evidences that you are facing oppositions.

The Scripture says in Gen 37:18-20

> *18 They saw him from afar, and before he came near them, they conspired against him to kill him. 19 They said to one another, "Here comes the dreamer. 20 Come now, let us kill him and throw him into one of the pits. Then we will say that a fierce animal has devoured him, and we will see what will become of his dreams.*

Each step Joseph took, there were obstacles that could have discouraged him to let go of his dream. In Genesis 37, when he went to give food to his brothers, they conspired to kill him. Though Reuben, in a bid to save and return his brother to their father, told his younger brothers to throw Joseph into a pit instead of killing him, they would later sell him to the Midianites merchantmen that passed by to Egypt. In all these, there was no mention of any form of reluctance or fight-back from Joseph. Joseph was sold for twenty pieces of silver. The Midianites took Joseph to Egypt and sold him to Potiphar, an officer of Pharaoh and a captain of the guard.

In Genesis 39 and verse 2, the bible says, the Lord was with Joseph and prospered him, though he was a slave in the house of his master. This means that prosperity is more than money. A man that carries the presence of God is prosperous. Little wonder, his master saw that presence and made him overseer over his house. The blessing of the Lord came upon the house of Potiphar because of Joseph. This means that every believer that is working for an unbeliever carries the blessing of the Lord and because of you, the business will prosper.

However, Potiphar's wife, who saw only the physical qualities of Joseph, chose to take advantage of the Hebrew slave and sleep with him. But Joseph resisted her proposition continually until she lied against him and was then thrown into prison. I don't know what you think about this, but to me, the whole process looked so discouraging and disappointing. Serving God and following His commandments should not lead you into trouble. Isn't it? God should rise and defend you, right? But Joseph, undeterred by these discouraging events, encouraged himself and continued trusting God.

Born To Dream

The presence of God followed him to the prison. And soon enough, he was again made the head of the prisoners. While there, he met two of Pharaoh's staff – the baker and the butler. They had a dream each and Joseph interpreted the dreams for them. He told the baker he would be killed in 3 days and the butler would be restored to his office in 3 days. He also told the butler to remember him after he has been restored to his position, but the butler forgot him until after two years when Pharaoh had a strange dream.

Joseph remained faithful at his work as the head of the prisoners. Never was it mentioned that he was disappointed in God for making him suffer unjustly for what he did not do. Several times the devil gets us to a point where we sin against God by complaining and doubting His might and capabilities. On occasions like this, our reactions and feelings are primarily based on our timing – when we expect God to show up. However, Joseph's story shows that we need to hold on and trust God because He is never late.

After Pharaoh had his dreams and no magician could interpret them, the butler remembered and told Pharaoh about Joseph. Pharaoh immediately sent for Joseph. I want you to see the expectation of Joseph. The Bible says in Gen 41:14

Then Pharaoh sent and called Joseph, and they quickly brought him out of the pit. And when he had shaved himself and changed his clothes, he came in before Pharaoh.

How can someone who is hastily brought out of prison have the time to shave and change his clothing? It must have been that Joseph had an expectation. I perceived that Joseph was expecting that, someday, he would be called to see Pharaoh and had rehearsed what he would do when the time comes.

I believe there were two things that helped Joseph go through this ordeal. The first one was his attitude. We never saw that Joseph complained either to God or to the people around him. In Genesis 39:2-4, the Bible says:

The LORD was with Joseph, and he became a successful man, and he was in the house of his Egyptian master. 3 His master saw that the LORD was with him and that the LORD caused all that he did to succeed in his hands. 4 So Joseph found favor in his sight and attended him, and he made him overseer of his house and put him in charge of all that he had.

Joseph did not lament over things, but kept his mind on God and His things. As a matter of fact, people noticed that God was with him. The grace of God on Joseph made his service exceptional. Everywhere he went, this grace was noticed as he was promoted to the highest offices. God's presence ensured that he prospered wherever he was. Joseph served faithfully both in the house of Potiphar and in prison and that ultimately led to him being faithful as a Prime Minister. The Bible says in Luke 16:12

And if you have not been faithful in that which is another's, who will give you that which is your own?

Joseph was faithful even in times of adversity and God blessed him with his own. It's quite interesting that Joseph looked for opportunities to be a blessing while still going through the most trying times of his life. Several of us will not want to help others when things are not going well for us. Joseph's attitude was different. He was ready to help others fulfill their dream while he waited in faith for God to fulfill His. He interpreted the dreams of the baker and the butler. He never did these for personal gain. That was why, even as a Prime Minister, he empowered people to make choices and did not manipulate things to his advantage.

The second thing that helped Joseph go through this ordeal was the presence of the Lord. The Scripture says in Genesis 39:21-23,

But the LORD was with Joseph and showed him steadfast love and gave him favor in the sight of the keeper of the prison. 22 And the keeper of the prison put Joseph in charge of all the prisoners who were in the prison. Whatever was done there, he

was the one who did it. 23 The keeper of the prison paid no attention to anything that was in Joseph's charge, because the LORD was with him. And whatever he did, the LORD made it succeed.

In these verses, we see that Joseph still carried a strong unction of God's presence. He was in tune with God, and sustained his communication with Him. Joseph never for once walked away from the presence of God. It is quite interesting that despite the things that Joseph went through he was still able to keep and cherish the presence of the Lord. Even when he was at Potiphar's house, the presence of the Lord made the difference. Among the slaves of his master, Joseph was different, and his case was also different. When he was thrown into prison, his case was also different. Remember the case of Job, when he went through his ordeal, his wife told him to curse God and die (Job 2:9). Unlike Job's wife, Joseph never sinned against God and his relationship with God was intact. In most instances, we are most vulnerable when we are going through challenges because, that is when we turn our back on God. I perceived that when Joseph went through this challenge, he worshiped God the more, he prayed to God the more, and he communed with God the more.

CHAPTER SIX

A GOD-SIZED DREAM: LIVING UP TO YOUR DREAM

The evidence of your belief is what we hear from your mouth.

Now to him who is able to do far more abundantly than all that we ask or think, according to the power at work within us.

Ephesians 3:20

In common English, the word faith literally means to take a risk. When someone takes a risk, there is the possibility of exposure to danger. This danger can be exposure to a loss or to something more unsettling. However, you must believe your dream enough to make some tangible movements towards its realization irrespective of the associated risk or harm. The journey to realizing your dreams begins with your willingness to take that step of faith. You need faith primarily because your God-inspired dream is God-sized. It's bigger than what you can ever imagine or ask. Your words or your imaginations have not yet been able to adequately convey or capture what God purposed to do through the dream He's given you.

Born To Dream

Several years ago, I knew I wanted to study Public Health outside the country where I was domiciled at the time. I believed it enough to let my wife know about my dream. At that time in her life, she was not interested in travelling out of our country of residence but at least, she knew what my dream was, and we prayed about it together. The dream was so real to me that everyone that came around me knew what my dream was. I spent a lot of time applying to several schools specifically in Europe because I thought that was where God wanted me to be. I started receiving positive responses from the schools I had sent applications. I got admissions into some of the schools but did not get funding. I believed the dream enough to keep applying even when I felt I personally did not have the funds to pay for the tuition. I knew what I wanted, and I kept doing what I thought I needed to do to actualize my dream.

So, you see, dreams don't just come to pass simply by conjuring up a big idea in our heads. Our words and actions must measure up to the dreams. In other words, you must live up to your dream to make it a reality. In this chapter, we will be looking at living up to your dream using the acronym ACT.

Born To Dream

1. Ask

In James 5:17, the Scripture says:

Elijah was a man with a nature like ours, and he prayed fervently that it might not rain, and for three years and six months it did not rain on the earth.

To ask simply means to pray. Your earnest desire is seen in how you pray. In other words, the bigger your dream, the more you should be praying, because you know that only God can bring that dream to pass. There is no way you can have a God-sized dream and not be praying about it. If you are not praying about it, it is just a sign that you believe you do not need God to accomplish it. Remember, if the dream is a big dream, it will only take the help of someone bigger and greater than you to fulfill it. Show me a man that wants something big and I will show you a man who is engaged in his secret courts.

Jesus came to save people from their sins. At the point where he was about birthing this dream, it was said that he prayed earnestly. He also asked his disciples to join him in prayers. In Matthew 26:40 the bible says

And he came to the disciples and found them sleeping. And he said to Peter, "So, could you not watch with me one hour?

Born To Dream

Jesus' expectation was that the disciple will be praying, but he came and found that they were deep in sleep. In Luke 22:44, the sweat from Jesus' head was like drops of blood. Jesus knew that only God could help him achieve that God-sized dream that He had.

Jabez was another example. He had quite a big dream. In the place of prayer, he engaged the help of the One who alone could bring the dream to pass. He prayed for the blessing of God to make him an honorable man. In 1 Chronicles 4:9-10, the Scripture sheds light on this story:

> *Jabez was more honorable than his brothers; and his mother called his name Jabez, saying, "Because I bore him in pain." 10 Jabez called upon the God of Israel, saying, "Oh that you would bless me and enlarge my border, and that your hand might be with me, and that you would keep me from harm so that it might not bring me pain!" And God granted what he asked.*

Jabez had a big dream where he saw himself as an honorable man, but everything around him was contrary to that dream. He knew that there was no way he could achieve that dream without God's help and he prayed to God to change his circumstances and the Lord did it.

For you to actualize a God-given dream, your actions in the place of prayer matters. If that dream is actually from God, then you need the help of the One who gave the dream to bring it to pass.

Also, we see a similar response in Jacob's story. He had stolen Esau's birthright, and as a result, now carrying the inheritance. But Jacob, in his current state as a con and a twister, cannot bear such responsibility. So, he fled the land of Canaan and stayed with his uncle for twenty years. There, God blessed him with two wives, many children, and wealth of servants, flock of sheep, goats and cattle. God then told him to go back to the land of Canaan. On his way back, the bible told us that he knew he was going to confront Esau and was sore afraid. Gripped with fear and uncertainty, Jacob leaned on God for help through his prayers.

In verses 24 to 26 of Genesis 32, he called unto God for help. The dream was just too big for him to fulfill that he knew he needed the help of God.

> *24 And Jacob was left alone; and there wrestled a man with him until the breaking of the day. 25 And when he saw that he prevailed not against him, he touched the hollow of his thigh; and the hollow of Jacob's thigh was out of joint, as he wrestled with him. 26 And he said, Let me go, for the day breaketh. And he said, I will not let thee go, except thou bless me. (KJV)*

Born To Dream

Jacob was not ready to let go until he received the blessing he needed. I really do not know how big your dreams are, but we serve a big God who will bring those dreams to pass when you engage him in the place of prayer.

2. Confess

A man that has a dream must be seen to confess it in his words. What are you saying you may ask? I told us of how I had a dream to study Public Health. The dream was so real to me that I told everyone that cared to hear. Even those who also did not care to hear about it, still heard it from me. It just wasn't possible to come around me and not hear about this dream that I had. The second important key to living up to your God-sized dream is your confession. In Mark 11:22-24, the Scripture says

> *22And Jesus answered them, "Have faith in God. 23 Truly, I say to you, whoever says to this mountain, 'Be taken up and thrown into the sea,' and does not doubt in his heart, but believes that what he says will come to pass, it will be done for him. 24 Therefore I tell you, whatever you ask in prayer, believe that you have received it, and it will be yours.*

In these verses of scripture, say or sayeth occurred six times. Note that God never repeats a word because He lacks what to say. In this verse, God was pointing our attention to the words He said repeatedly. In this context, it shows that what you say matters. A man that has a big dream must keep confessing it. There's a popular saying that a shut mouth is a shut destiny. Sometimes, the enemy uses the size of our dream to intimidate us into silence. So, when we come around people, we are afraid of telling them about that big dream because they may laugh at us.

When God told Noah to build an ark, people must have laughed him to scorn. At that time, it had not rained yet, not to talk of flooding the earth and destroying it. The concept of rain falling on the earth was not something that had been seen. And there you have someone building an ark. It was simply illogical. But Noah won't be deterred by all that. So, he kept building and following what God showed him without giving heed to the objections from the people.

Remember, it was the dreams that God gave Joseph that he spoke about. He believed it enough to speak out. I know some people would encourage you to keep quiet so that the devil doesn't get to know about the dream and somehow scuttle it. But on the contrary, I beg to say that no man carries fire in his bosom and keeps quiet. If Joseph had kept quiet, his brothers would not have heard him. If his brothers did not hear him, he would not have been thrown in the pit. If he was not thrown in the pit, he would not have been sold. If he was not sold, he would not have found himself in Potiphar's house. And it goes on and on until he found himself in the palace. His words never changed; he kept saying what he saw from the beginning. The evidence of your belief is what we hear from your mouth.

Born To Dream

Some people would say something positive in their closet and when they come before people, they begin to engage in negative confessions. That is not only wrong but also cancels the positive confessions you made in your closet. You need to be consistent in your confession. You cannot be spewing hot and cold at the same time.

Romans 10:9-10 says:

> *9 That if thou shalt confess with thy mouth the Lord Jesus, and shalt believe in thine heart that God hath raised him from the dead, thou shalt be saved. 10 For with the heart man believeth unto righteousness; and with the mouth confession is made unto salvation.* (KJV)

You must always learn to confess the dream in your heart and not the fear in your head. Confessing the fear in your head will ultimately open the gateway of your heart to it. And once fear grips your heart, it suffocates and kills your dream. You always have a choice about what you say. Keep confessing the right things and sooner than later, those dreams will come to pass. As I said earlier, it is often said that "a shut mouth is a shut destiny," so, learn to speak out. In Hebrews 10:23 the bible says:

> *Let us hold fast the confession of our hope without wavering, for he who promised is faithful.*

Born To Dream

One of the areas where the devil takes advantage of Christians is in confession. Many Christians don't spend time confessing their dreams. In Genesis 1, God, who is the greatest dreamer, spoke what He saw internally, and it came to pass externally. He did not complain about the chaos or even the darkness. Instead, He spoke what He wanted to see. Your words should be faith-filled and not fear-filled.

3. Time

The final item in acting to the size of your dream is time. Time is the crucible through which your dream will be tested. Joseph had a dream, and for seventeen years he did not ascend. Rather, he was in pits and prison until he finally ascended the throne at the age of 30. David, on the other hand, spent about 15 years rearing sheep at the backside of the desert and playing fugitive before he ascended the throne as the King of Judah. Folks, time will test your belief in your dream. Remember, Abraham waited 25 years for the Word of God over his life to come to pass. During that period, he had Ishmael, thinking that the promised child was going to come from Haggai, his maid. You must be willing to wait on God to bring your dream to manifest, no matter how long it takes. Yes, you might make some mistakes while waiting like Abraham, but you must still hold on to the dream.

Born To Dream

Be encouraged that God is not a man. He will keep to His word. Any dream that God cannot fulfill, He will definitely not show you.

Chapter Seven

MAINTAINING THE LIFE OF A DREAMER

The dreams God shares with us are products of the boundless intelligence of the creative God. So, there's no how we can comprehend its length and breadth in one fell swoop.

Now Joseph had a dream, and when he told it to his brothers, they hated him even more... 9 Then he dreamed another dream and told it to his brothers and said, "Behold, I have dreamed another dream. Behold, the sun, the moon, and eleven stars were bowing down to me."...11 And his brothers were jealous of him, but his father kept the saying in mind. (Genesis 37)

There are some dreams that are short-term, whereas others are long-term. For example, you may have a dream to be a doctor. As soon as you achieve it, that dream is accomplished. In some instance, achieving that dream may pose some difficulties and may take a lot longer time than you had anticipated. Well, that is typical of dreams. However, I want to remind you to never give up on your dream. Instead, pursue your aspiration and, by the grace of God coupled with determination, you will achieve it.

It is important to know that the fulfillment of a dream is not necessarily the end of dreaming. You must maintain the life of a dreamer if the Lord has still given you breath in your nostrils.

In Acts 2:16-17, the Scripture says

> *But this is what was uttered through the prophet Joel: 17 "'And in the last days it shall be, God declares, that I will pour out my Spirit on all flesh, and your sons and your daughters shall prophesy, and your young men shall see visions, and your old men shall dream dreams;*

You must never get to a point where you think you are too old to dream or dream again. I know of a man who, in his eighties, started a business in 2022. What a dogged spirit that is! In his eighties, he is still dreaming and running with his dream. Some of us would have said "There is nothing much about life again. Let me just lie down and wait for my maker to call me home." Others might say, "Why start a business now when I am too old to oversee it, and may be gone anytime." But this man is still dreaming. Don't say you're too old to dream.

WHY MUST YOU MAINTAIN THE LIFE OF A DREAMER?

Born To Dream

There are quite a lot of reasons why a dreamer should continue to dream. In this chapter, I will discuss four reasons you should maintain the life of a dreamer.

1. A dream begets another dream

The truth is that, several other dreams can be embedded within a single dream. As the dream unfolds, you begin to dream other dreams. The manifestation of one dream allows you to dream multiple other dreams. A perfect example to illustrate this is a seed. In one seed of orange lie hundreds of other orange seeds. If you sow this single orange seed, cater for it until it matures and begins to produce fruits, you can be certain to have a thousand-fold returns on your investment. It's the same thing with dreams. One dream opens the doors to multiple new dreams.

2. You do not see the full picture

God-sized dreams are too lofty for our fragile and limited minds to fully grasp or comprehend. The dreams God shares with us are products of the boundless intelligence of the creative God. So, there's no how we can comprehend its length and breadth in one fell swoop. What happens therefore, is that the dream unfolds as we journey on, and we begin to see things we had never seen or imagined. In most instances, God shows us the end from the beginning. So, the once hid in-betweens begin to open up to us. So, you must not halt this dreamer life that you've embraced.

3. The life of a righteous man shines better

There is something about your tomorrow that is better and greater than your today. In Proverbs 4:18, the Scripture says

But the path of the righteous is like the light of dawn, which shines brighter and brighter until full day.

As a righteous man, God expects your tomorrow to be better than your today. So, don't think or assume you've seen it all. God is not finished with you yet. So, don't stop dreaming.

4. The dream of someone is tied to your own dream

It is quite interesting that dreams are intertwined. In many instances, as you help people fulfill their dreams, it opens a door for the fulfillment of your dream also. In the book of Luke 16:12, the Bible says

And if you have not been faithful in that which is another's, who will give you that which is your own?

When you are faithful in another man's business God gives you the opportunity to get your dream fulfilled. I remember at a certain time in my life, I was helping a colleague to look for a place to start a business. My intention wasn't to start my own business, but that process led to me starting my own business. It opened an opportunity for me to dream just because I was helping someone else fulfill her dream.

GOD AT THE CENTER

While it is important to keep dreaming, we must remind ourselves of the crucial role of God in all these. For you to fulfill your dreams, it is important you obey God's instructions. God creates a picture in your mind. That picture needs to come to fruition. But it will take God to birth that dream. The key to birthing that dream is your obedience to the instructions you have received from God. I have discovered that for each new level God is taking you to, there are instructions for you to obey. Most times, it comes in the form of giving or sacrifice.

Hebrews 11:17-19

> *By faith Abraham, when he was tested, offered up Isaac, and he who had received the promises was in the act of offering up his only son, 18 of whom it was said, "Through Isaac shall your offspring be named." 19 He considered that God was able even to raise him from the dead, from which, figuratively speaking, he did receive him back.*

Abraham was willing to obey God's instruction by giving up his son. He believed that God was able to bring him back from the dead. We speak so much about grace as an unmerited favor, but grace is also an enablement to do. What we could not do, Jesus did, and through Him, we have the enablement to do.

Philippians 2:12 says

> *Therefore, my beloved, as you have always obeyed, so now, not only as in my presence but much more in my absence, work out your own salvation with fear and trembling, 13 for it is God who works in you, both to will and to work for his good pleasure.*

In this verse of scripture, Paul admonishes us (by way of application) to work out our salvation with fear and trembling. However, in verse 13, Paul goes further to let us know that God is the one working in us both to will and to do of His good pleasure. In other words, what we are working out can only be what has been worked out in us by God. We cannot do anything, but by the grace of God. Think about that for a moment. God is actively at work in your heart, producing the willingness and the action that follows in carrying out deeds that bring Him great pleasure. This revelation is critical to your fulfillment of the dreams that God has deposited in your heart.

Chapter Eight

WAITING ON YOUR DREAMS

God uses the time of waiting to prepare us with every capacity –
mental, spiritual, and physical – needed to receive and nurture the
blessings.

But these things I plan won't happen right away. Slowly,
steadily, surely, the time approaches when the vision will be
fulfilled. If it seems slow, do not despair, for these things will
surely come to pass. Just be patient! They will not be overdue a
single day! Habakkuk 2:3 (Living Bible)

Joseph was a young man who had dreams and expectations from God. But interestingly, they did not come to pass immediately. Between the dream, aspirations and goals, there is a waiting time. How do I maximize the time-period between when God speaks and the materialization of the dream?

It took Abraham twenty-five years for the prophecy to be fulfilled (Genesis 12:1-4; 21:1-5). David was anointed king at the age of 15, but he had to wait until about the age of thirty before he became Israel's king (1 Sam 16:1-3). Joseph's story was not different. He had his dreams at about the age of seventeen and they were fulfilled at thirty years of age (Gen 37:6-9). Noah also waited one hundred and twenty years from the time he started building the ark until it began to rain (Genesis 5:32; 7:6). God told Moses he would lead his people out of Egypt, where they had spent the last four hundred years in slavery. But then, God made him to wait (and learn servant leadership) in the desert for forty years. Even Jesus waited until he became thirty years old before he began his ministry – He waited another eighteen years from the time he taught in the synagogue at age 12.

So, why the wait? In the next few paragraphs, I will attempt to provide some answers to this question. Now, let's get started.

1. God prepares us in the Wait

I believe that one of the reasons we have to wait is not because God is testing us, as we have been made to believe. On the contrary, God uses the time of waiting to prepare us with every capacity – mental, spiritual, and physical – needed to receive and nurture the blessings. God wants to work on you before he releases His blessing upon you. The time of waiting is a time of preparation. The blessing is glory, and every glory comes with a weight. A man that is not prepared will crash under its weight at the time of his glorification. This is why some people fall when they get to the peak of their lives. The glory is so great, that they are carried away by it.

2. The waiting period is the period of Concealment

A seed must first die before it comes alive and flourishes. During this period of concealment, nobody sees you. Jesus was taken to Egypt so that He would not be killed by Herod. David hid in caves as fugitive and was a shepherd boy at the backside of the desert. Between the ages of 12-30 years, nothing was said about Jesus until he was baptized in the river Jordan. The waiting period is the time of concealment or obscurity. It protects and keeps you from the visibility of dream killers and allows you to mature out of their sight.

3. It builds our trust and faith in God

The waiting period is also a time for us to build our faith and trust in God. This is because the dream we received from God will be proved. How do we know that you believe the dream if it is not proved? As mentioned earlier, it takes both God and us for our dreams to be fulfilled. What we see during your waiting period will show us if you believe the dream or not. Sometimes, we claim we believe the dream, but as time passes, our faith in the dream weakens and fades away. The waiting period gives you the opportunity to deepen your trust in God and build a robust relationship with Him.

4. Manifestation is based on God's time and not our time

We must understand that the timing of our dreams is based on God and Him only. He holds the timing of our lives. Since the unfolding of the events is in God's hand, we wait on God for its fulfillment. In Ecclesiastes 3:11, the Bible says:

He has made everything beautiful in its time. Also, he has put eternity into man's heart, yet so that he cannot find out what God has done from the beginning to the end.

It is now clear that the waiting period is not necessarily a bad time. Because of how crucial this period is, it is important that you know how to wait.

HOW DO YOU WAIT?

1. In Prayer and Fasting

The waiting time should be spent in prayer and fasting, seeking the face of God. If we say that we need the help of God to fulfill our dream, then we must engage Him to receive that help. We also need to receive direction to know the next steps to take. As a result, we must devote ourselves to fasting and praying.

2. In Faith

The scripture says in several places that "the just shall live by faith." While we wait for the fulfillment of our dreams, we must live daily believing God to bring them to pass. Our faith is that evidence that we bring forth, to demonstrate that we believe the dream.

3. In Patience

James (5:10-11) and Hebrews (6:12) teach us that patience is a virtue. Sadly, this virtue is missing in our days. Everyone – young and old, men and women, rich and poor – wants to get their dreams fulfilled now. Those who wait, wait in patience. Patience is a fruit of the Spirit that we all need as Christians. When we wait on God to fulfill our dreams, we should wait in patience for him to do what He purposed to do.

4. By Helping Others

I remember several years ago, when I trusted God to do something for my family and me. While waiting, I was helping other people fulfill the same dream in their lives. In Luke 10, we see the story of the Good Samaritan. This story has some instructive lessons about helping others.

It is quite interesting that there were three people that passed by the injured man – the Priest, the Levite and the Samaritan. You would have expected the Priest or the Levite to help the man, but it was the Samaritan that did. This shows us a great lesson here: ordinary people can do and achieve extraordinary results. Sometimes, we look down on ourselves, saying we cannot do it. But in this story, you can see someone who has no position or title doing something great. It also shows that most times, things don't always turn out to be what we think they are.

Remember when Samuel was anointing the sons of Jesse. He had thought the first born was the king based on how he looked. But he was not the chosen one. Samuel was wrong!

In Luke 10 from verse 30, Jesus said a man was traveling from Jerusalem to Jericho and was robbed by thieves who striped him naked and left him half dead. The Priest and the Levite all passed him by, but the Samaritan took certain actions (that I will enumerate below) to help the stranger. There are certain things mentioned in verse 34 that are worth mentioning, about how the Good Samaritan helped the man.

Luke 10:34

And went to him, and bound up his wounds, pouring in oil and wine, and set him on his own beast, and brought him to an inn, and took care of him.

1. He went to him

This means that he connected with him. He initiated the movement to go to the stranger and connected to him. Most times, for us to connect to people, we must look for common grounds while we recognize and respect our differences. Don't take anyone for granted. The fact that they are down today, does not mean that they will forever be down.

2. Bound up his wounds

This connotes empathy. He understood what the man was going through that he was willing to stop the bleeding. How many people will see you bleed today and be willing to help stop it? I am sure it would be all over the social media. The man was vulnerable, but he was not exploited. It was John Maxwell that said "People do not care how much you know until they know how much you care."

3. Pour oil/wine

This connotes faith in people. The Good Samaritan had so much faith in the man that he poured olive oil, and wine to disinfect the wound. We need to believe in people to the extent that we are ready to act in their favor. Several people do not believe in themselves and therefore, find it difficult to believe in others. Our world today needs people who can look beyond people's present predicament and believe in them. We are so suspicious of others that we leave no room for mistakes.

4. Set him on his beast

The Good Samaritan then carried this man and put him on his beast. He empowered the man by lifting him up. Several people want to help others but not necessarily to enlarge or empower them They are willing to help you but not to bring you to their level. If you are still down there, they are comfortable. However, the Samaritan made him to ride on the same beast he was riding. Some of us can't even allow our protégé drive our cars. Jesus could have rebuked Peter when he asked if he could walk on water, but instead he encouraged him.

5. Brought him to an inn

This speaks of nurturing. He created a safe environment for him to heal. You must learn to give people the right environment to grow and love them unconditionally. You cannot make a person feel important in your presence if, in the secret, you feel they are nobody.

6. Took care of him

This means he paid for the bills. The amount you are willing to pay for a thing shows the value you place on that thing. He paid the bills and promised to pay for any other bill that may be incurred. Please invest your time, money and or talent in impacting the lives of people; it is worth it.

The truth is, we cannot help others get to the top without being at the top also. Look for opportunities to help people in need. By doing so, you're setting the stage for your greatness.

CHAPTER NINE

GOD. DREAMS. YOU

Without God, as this Scripture shows, everything is void, empty, without form, or purpose. God is the author of purpose – for every created thing and every human.

From the book of Genesis, God's intention to build a perfect world was very clear. With chaos and darkness at the reins, God stepped in and fashioned a world after His dream. God's inestimable power and greatness was demonstrated in the creation story of the Bible. Pretty much quickly, we found God at work. The first action word in the Bible that conveys God's identity was "created."

> *In the beginning, God created the heavens and the earth.* Genesis 1:1 (ESV)

It was God we first saw. Not anyone else. And we saw Him creating. There was no way He could have created something that was not already inside of Him. God is the Master dreamer; the One from whom every believer draws their dreams.

GOD IN THE CHAOS

Soon after we saw God creating the heavens and the earth in Genesis 1:1, the second verse shows a world that was steeped in darkness.

> *The earth was without form and void, and darkness was over the face of the deep. And the Spirit of God was hovering over the face of the waters.* Genesis 1:2 (ESV)

In a sudden twist of a tale, the darkness was over the surface of the waters. But that's not all. There was also emptiness – void. Nothing truly takes its right form where darkness rules. Without God, as this Scripture shows, everything is void, empty, without form, or purpose. God is the author of purpose – for every created thing and every human. We did not see anyone or anything else. We see only God. So, no matter the success a man records in life, without God all such successes mean nothing. They are void, and formless.

It is no wonder why depression and suicidal inclinations are not solely the problems of the poor. The rich of this world, despite their material comfort and societal influence, still experience some form of emptiness and hopelessness. Their riches are not able to insulate them from hopeless thoughts. Their library of awards and achievements cannot fill the void in their hearts. Only God can. So, without God, dreams and aspirations and feats mean nothing. God is the one who confers us with the "somebody" status. Jesus affirmed this when He told the disciples, in John 15:5, that

> *I am the vine; you are the branches. If you remain in me and I in you, you will bear much fruit; apart from me you can do nothing.*

So, when God steps into chaos, he establishes order. When He steps into darkness, light takes residence. The presence of God in chaos means life, light, hope, and love, aligning everything with the will and purpose of God. God invites us to partake in His creation venture through the avenue of dreams. That is why He shares His eternal purpose in our hearts via dreams.

When God wanted to preserve His people, the sons of Jacob (and the people of the world), he placed a dream in the heart of Joseph, and orchestrated his journey to Egypt. And at the appointed time, God fulfilled the dream he had shared with Joseph many years before. Through the dream, God created order and organization where chaos could have ruled.

Thus, the chaotic earth finds order when God steps into it. Today, God continues to step into the world's chaotic situations. And just like He did through Joseph, God is stepping into the disorderliness of our world through us, His sons and daughters. God's eternal purpose to firmly make the earth His Kingdom is conveyed to us through the vehicle of dreams. He tells us what he wants to do on earth through us.

Born To Dream

In Genesis, when God wanted to bless the world, He revealed it to Abraham, that by his seed, the entire human race would be blessed. Abraham caught this vision, and ran with it.

> *I will surely bless you, and I will surely multiply your offspring as the stars of heaven and as the sand that is on the seashore. And your offspring shall possess the gate of his enemies, 18 and in your offspring shall all the nations of the earth be blessed, because you have obeyed my voice.* Genesis 22:17-18 (ESV)

Is there chaos in your community? Are things falling outside of God's plan for your community? Is there a problem that has plagued the people so long in your nation? If yes, then be rest assured that God is looking for people like you through whom He would step into these chaotic situations. God looks for a dreamer, willing to run with the vision of heaven. God, like it has always been, is looking for people with a receptive mind to carry, birth, and nurture His dreams on earth.

In Genesis 1:26-28, God created something that perfectly reflected who He is. But before creating the man, the Godhead had a clear picture of who they wanted to create. The dream was plain and unambiguous in the mind of God.

> *26 Then God said, "Let us make man in our image, after our likeness. And let them have dominion over the fish of the sea and over the birds of the heavens and over the livestock and over all*

the earth and over every creeping thing that creeps on the earth." 27 So God created man in his own image, in the image of God he created him; male and female he created them. 28 And God blessed them. And God said to them, "Be fruitful and multiply and fill the earth and subdue it, and have dominion over the fish of the sea and over the birds of the heavens and over every living thing that moves on the earth."

In creating humans, God fashioned us after His image – sharing certain divine attributes with us – just as He had dreamed. One of such attributes is the capacity to dream and create. God dreamt, and Adam was created! Then He thought that the first man He created was helpless and without a suitable companion. So, He made a woman suitable for him. With the picture and purpose conceived, God created a woman that perfectly suits Adam's need of a companion and helper.

It is, therefore, safe to say that no human is a product of chance. About human identity, someone wrote this:

"You are a strategic idea in the eternal mind of God, long before creation, that was uniquely crafted and birthed in calculated time."

It doesn't matter how you were conceived, God had you in His mind all along, even before the foundation of the earth was put in place. You're not a mistake. And God doesn't create mistakes. God created you with the capacity to dream big dreams like Him.

DREAM ALL YOU WANT – THE WORLD IS YOURS

You see, when people dream, they're only showing their divine attributes. When you dream, you show that you are a bona fide child of God. Dreaming is the normal Christian way of life. When we dream of making a place better, we should remember we're only replicating the nature of our Father in Heaven. So, don't be afraid to dream the impossible. Don't let anyone or anything stop you from dreaming. The world is yours for the taking. And like Abraham, you can take as much land as you can see. God is a big dreamer. So also, should you be. Don't let your past failures, present realities, or uncertainties of tomorrow keep you back. Break free from every yoke that holds you bound. Dream big. Dream like God does. After all, you're created in the image of God.

Like I quoted earlier, you are a strategic idea in God's eternal mind. And God birthed you precisely for a purpose. You must uncover that purpose and run with it. There cannot be a greater joy in life than living a life that you're designed to live. You cannot be anything greater than what you've been designed to be. Everything about you is fashioned to serve a higher purpose – a divine purpose. If you live outside of your purpose, the best you will be is second best. And you would have missed out on the incredible things God planned to do with and through your life.

Born To Dream

When Ford, Lamborghini, or Mercedes-Benz engineers set out to create a prototype automobile, every part of that vehicle is designed and created to serve certain purposes. If, however, they are used only to serve an aesthetic purpose, they'd have lived below their capacities and purposes. Or if the owner uses the vehicle only when they want to listen to music, the vehicle's purpose wouldn't have been maximized. As long as the owner does not understand the vehicle's many functions, they would under-utilize it.

Like the automobile example, when you don't realize that God's ultimate purpose for your life is to bring to disrepute the kingdom of darkness and propagate the Kingdom of YHWH on earth, you'd have lived far below your purpose. God made you for a nobler purpose than the devil or your current circumstances and limitations would make you believe. No self-help therapy will help you either. It is the One who created you in the first place that can fully reveal your life's purpose.

God is at the center of it all – the dreams and you. God is the one who created you for that specific purpose. And it's by looking God-ward that you can fully grasp why on earth you're here. So, it doesn't matter how big your dreams are, if they fall outside of God's purpose, they make no eternal meaning. That is why you must take a look at your dreams again against the characteristics of a God-given dream (see Chapter One). God does not intend to give you a dream that serves your interest only. He gives you a dream that is as big as Him; dreams that will transcend you and your generations. Just like God blessed the entire world through the seed of Abraham, God wants to bless the world through you. That's why you should open up your mind and let the Lord plant His dream right in your heart.

Let God reveal His purpose to you. Let His Word landscape your heart, setting you on the path of dreaming dreams that align with divine agenda for your life. God is the giver of dreams. You are the one to execute the dreams. God is committed to sharing His dreams with you. The only question is: Are you prepared to conceive and run with them?

CHAPTER TEN

MEN AND WOMEN WHO DARED TO DREAM

Don't rest on yesterday's successes, and don't be daunted by the fears that come with tomorrow. Maximize every opportunity you have today, and lean on God to fulfill the dream he has put in your heart. The world waits for the manifestation of your dreams.

Throughout the pages of this book, I have only done one thing: inspire you to dream big and live the life of your dream. This call is not an impossible call. As we saw in the many biblical stories I shared in the previous chapters, dreaming big and living out your dreams are not impossible. However, you may still nurture some doubts in your minds, saying "But these are examples of people from the Bible times." You may even be skeptical about the idea that these stories happened in real human time. Without invalidating your concerns, I'll like to affirm to you that these biblical events happened in verifiable human time, most of which recent archeological expeditions have confirmed to have occurred. However, connecting these biblical truths to contemporary time will serve to further boost your faith and confidence in God and the capacity He has endowed you with. As a result, in this chapter, we would focus on stories of men and women who, against all odds, made an impact on their generations by following their dreams. It is my hope that this serves to strengthen your faith and energize you to pursue your dreams to fulfillment.

BEN CARSON

Ben Carson's story is one of remarkable resilience and determination. He was born into poverty in Detroit, Michigan, in 1951, and raised by a single mother who had only a third-grade education. Despite facing significant challenges in his childhood, Ben was determined to succeed and make something of himself.

As a child, Ben struggled academically and was often teased by his classmates for being the "dumbest kid in class." But his mother, Sonya, refused to let her son believe he was not smart. She encouraged him to read and pushed him to work harder in school. She even required him to read two library books a week and write reports on them, even though she herself was illiterate.

Ben's hard work paid off, and he began to excel in school. He eventually earned a scholarship to Yale University, where he majored in psychology. After graduating from Yale, he attended the University of Michigan Medical School, where he developed a passion for neurosurgery.

Ben's career as a neurosurgeon was nothing short of exceptional. He was the first surgeon to successfully separate conjoined twins who were joined at the head, and he performed numerous other groundbreaking surgeries throughout his career. He also became a professor of neurosurgery, and authored several books on his experiences as a doctor and as a patient.

Despite his many accomplishments, Ben never forgot where he came from. He remained humble and grateful for the opportunities he had been given, and he used his success to give back to others. He established the Carson Scholars Fund, which provides scholarships to students who excel academically and demonstrate a commitment to serving their communities.

VIVIEN THOMAS

Vivien Thomas was a man who overcame seemingly insurmountable obstacles to achieve greatness in the field of medicine. Born in 1910 in Louisiana, Vivien grew up in a world where racism and segregation were the norm. But these limited opportunities occasioned by his race did not define Vivien or stop him from dreaming big.

Born To Dream

After finishing high school, Vivien moved to Nashville, Tennessee, where he hoped to pursue a career in medicine. However, due to his family's financial situation, he was unable to afford college. An undeterred Vivien took a job as a lab assistant at Vanderbilt University, where he met Dr. Alfred Blalock, a renowned surgeon.

It didn't take long before Dr. Blalock recognized Vivien's intelligence and work ethic, and he soon offered him a job as his lab assistant at Johns Hopkins University in Baltimore. However, because of Jim Crow laws, Vivien was not allowed to attend medical school or be promoted to a position as a surgeon. Instead, he worked as a lab technician, performing surgeries on animals to help Dr. Blalock develop a groundbreaking procedure to treat a deadly heart defect called blue baby syndrome.

Vivien quickly became an expert in the field of surgery, even though he lacked formal training. He worked tirelessly, often spending countless hours in the lab perfecting surgical techniques and devising new tools and instruments to help Dr. Blalock perform the life-saving procedure.

In 1944, after years of hard work, Vivien and Dr. Blalock successfully performed the first blue baby operation on a human patient. The surgery was a resounding success and marked a turning point in the field of heart surgery.

Vivien's contributions to the field of medicine were significant, yet he remained largely unrecognized for his work until many years later. However, Vivien Thomas remains a shining example of what can be achieved when we have the courage to pursue our dreams, even without accolades or recognition.

THOMAS EDISON

Thomas Edison was a man who refused to let failure stand in the way of his dreams. Born in 1847 in Milan, Ohio, Edison was a curious and ambitious child who showed a keen interest in science and technology from a young age.

Edison remained determined to pursue his passion for inventing despite struggling in school due to undiagnosed hearing loss. He worked tirelessly on various projects, often spending hours in his makeshift laboratory conducting experiments and testing new ideas.

His first major invention was the phonograph, which he developed in 1877. The phonograph was a revolutionary device that allowed people to record and play back sound for the first time. This invention catapulted Edison to fame and established him as a leading inventor in the field of technology.

However, Edison's success did not come without setbacks. He faced numerous failures and setbacks throughout his career, often spending months or even years working on projects that ultimately proved unsuccessful. But rather than giving up, Edison saw each failure as an opportunity to learn and improve.

One of Edison's most famous quotes is, "I have not failed. I've just found 10,000 ways that won't work." This attitude of perseverance and resilience helped him achieve many more successes throughout his career, including the invention of the electric light bulb, the motion picture camera, and the storage battery.

Edison's legacy as a pioneering inventor and entrepreneur continues to inspire people around the world to dream big and have the courage to pursue their dreams. His willingness to take risks and try new things, even in the face of uncertainty and doubt, helped him achieve greatness and change the world for the better.

THE NASA WOMEN

Mary Jackson, Katherine Johnson, and Dorothy Vaughan, popularly referred to as The NASA Women, were three African-American women who defied the odds and made history at NASA during a time when segregation and discrimination were rampant.

Mary Jackson was born in Virginia in 1921 and graduated from Hampton Institute with a degree in mathematics and physical science. Despite facing discrimination and limited opportunities due to her race and gender, Mary was determined to pursue her dream of becoming an engineer. She joined NASA's predecessor, the National Advisory Committee for Aeronautics (NACA), in 1951 and became the first African American woman engineer at the agency.

Katherine Johnson was born in West Virginia in 1918 and excelled in mathematics from a young age. She attended West Virginia State College and eventually began working at NACA in 1953. Katherine's incredible mathematical skills helped her become one of the key figures in the space program, calculating trajectories for space missions including the first manned spaceflight in 1961 and the Apollo 11 mission to the moon in 1969.

Dorothy Vaughan was born in Missouri in 1910 and earned a degree in mathematics from Wilberforce University. She began working at NACA in 1943 as a "computer," a job that involved manually performing complex calculations. However, when the agency began transitioning to electronic computers, Dorothy saw an opportunity to learn new skills and become an expert in computer programming. She led a team of female African American programmers and played a key role in the successful launch of the first American satellite in 1958.

In the face of discrimination and segregation at work and in their personal lives, these three women refused to abandon their dreams because of their circumstances. They worked tirelessly to overcome obstacles and pursue their passions, paving the way for future generations of women and people of color in the fields of science, technology, engineering, and mathematics (STEM).

Their inspiring story was immortalized in the book and movie *Hidden Figures*, which brought their incredible achievements to light and inspired countless people around the world to follow in their footsteps.

NELLIE BLY

Nellie Bly was a trailblazing journalist and adventurer who proved that anything is possible with determination and a willingness to take risks. Born Elizabeth Cochran in Pennsylvania in 1864, Nellie was an intelligent and curious child who dreamed of becoming a writer. However, her family's financial struggles meant that Nellie had to drop out of school and work as a factory girl to help support them.

These challenges, however, did not deter her from following her dream through. She began writing for a local newspaper under the pseudonym "Nellie Bly" and quickly gained a reputation for her hard-hitting investigative journalism.

In 1887, Nellie made headlines when she pretended to be insane in order to get herself committed to the Women's Lunatic Asylum on Blackwell's Island. Her exposé on the inhumane treatment of patients at the asylum sparked public outrage and led to sweeping reforms in the mental health system.

But Nellie's adventures didn't stop there. In 1889, she set out on a journey around the world to beat the fictional record of Phileas Fogg from Jules Verne's novel *Around the World in 80 Days*. Nellie traveled by ship, train, and even elephant, and her journey captured the imagination of people around the world.

Throughout her career, Nellie faced numerous obstacles and challenges, including discrimination and sexism. But she refused to let these impediments discourage her from pursuing her dreams. Nellie Bly's fearless spirit and determination to make a difference have inspired generations of journalists and adventurers.

ALEXANDER GRAHAM BELL

Alexander Graham Bell is remembered as one of the greatest inventors in history. Born in Scotland in 1847, Bell was fascinated by sound and communication from a young age. He worked tirelessly to develop new technologies and devices that would allow people to communicate over long distances.

However, Bell's early efforts were met with little success. He spent years experimenting with various devices and technologies, but none of them worked as well as he hoped. He struggled to find funding for his projects, and he faced skepticism and criticism from many in the scientific community.

In the face of these difficulties, Bell refused to give up on his dreams. He continued to work tirelessly, experimenting with different materials and techniques until he finally stumbled upon the breakthrough he had been searching for.

In 1876, Bell patented the telephone, a device that revolutionized communication and changed the world forever. His invention was met with widespread acclaim, and he quickly became one of the most famous inventors in history.

ALBERT EINSTEIN

Albert Einstein is widely regarded as one of the greatest scientific minds in history, but his path to success was not an easy one. In fact, Einstein experienced numerous failures and setbacks throughout his life, which makes his story all the more inspiring.

Born in Germany in 1879, Einstein showed a keen interest in science and mathematics from a young age. However, his unconventional thinking and rebellious attitude often landed him in trouble at school, and he struggled to gain acceptance in the academic world.

Born To Dream

After graduating from college, Einstein spent several years working as a clerk in a patent office, where he had ample time to pursue his scientific interests on the side. He spent countless hours studying and experimenting, and he eventually developed his famous theory of relativity, which revolutionized the field of physics.

But even after achieving this incredible breakthrough, Einstein faced numerous challenges and setbacks. He struggled to gain acceptance in the scientific community, and many of his ideas were met with skepticism and criticism. But he remained committed to his work, and continued to innovate and explore new ideas throughout his life. He made numerous groundbreaking discoveries and contributions to science, becoming (arguably) the most famous and respected scientists in history.

Einstein's story is about more than just his incredible accomplishments; it's also about the power of dreaming, and persevering in spite of evident failures. Einstein failed numerous times throughout his life, but he never gave up on his dreams. Instead, he used his failures as opportunities to learn and grow, and he continued to pursue his passions with courage and tenacity.

Born To Dream

ANAND KUMAR

Anand Kumar is an Indian mathematician and educator who has dedicated his life to helping underprivileged students achieve their dreams. His story is a powerful reminder that our dreams are always bigger than us, and if we are willing to work hard, persevere through adversity, and believe in ourselves, we'll achieve them.

Born into a low-income family in India, Kumar was passionate about mathematics from a young age. However, his family's financial struggles made it difficult for him to pursue his studies, and he often had to rely on donations to fund his education. After solving a complex mathematical problem, Kumar was accepted into the prestigious Cambridge University but, again, finances stood in his way. Undeterred, Kumar began teaching mathematics to local children in his hometown of Patna.

Kumar quickly realized that many of these children were just as talented and passionate about mathematics as he was, but they lacked the resources and opportunities to develop their skills. Unwavering in his quest to make a difference, Kumar founded the Super 30 program in 2002. This program provides free coaching and support to underprivileged students who aspire to pursue careers in mathematics and science.

Born To Dream

Through the Super 30 program, Kumar has helped countless students overcome poverty and adversity and achieve their dreams. The program has a remarkable success rate, with nearly all of its graduates going on to prestigious universities and successful careers in their chosen fields.

Kumar's work has earned him numerous accolades and awards, and he has become a beloved figure in India's educational community. His story serves as a powerful inspiration to all those who dare to dream big and pursue their passions.

NICHOLAS JAMES VUJICIC

Nicholas James Vujicic, commonly known as Pastor Nick, is a motivational speaker, author, and pastor who has inspired millions of people around the world with his powerful message of hope, perseverance, and determination.

Born in Australia in 1982 to Christian parents, Nick was born without arms or legs due to a rare genetic condition called tetra-Amelia syndrome. As a child, he struggled to fit in and often felt isolated and alone. However, with the love and support of his family, he was able to overcome his limitations and embrace life to the fullest.

As a teenager, Nick discovered a passion for public speaking, and he began sharing his story with others in the hopes of inspiring them to overcome their own challenges. Despite facing a rainbow of rejections and setbacks, he refused to give up on his dreams, and he eventually became one of the most sought-after motivational speakers in the world.

Nick's message of hope and perseverance has resonated with people of all ages and backgrounds, and he has touched the lives of millions of people around the world. He has authored several bestselling books, including "*Life Without Limits*" and "*Unstoppable*," and he continues to inspire others with his powerful message of resilience and determination.

Through his own example, Nick has shown that anything is possible if we have the courage to dream big and believe in God (ourselves) to bring our dreams to reality. He has demonstrated that our limitations do not have to define us, and that with hard work, perseverance, and a positive attitude, we can overcome even the most challenging obstacles. Have you ever felt limited and held back by your circumstances? Nick's story serves as a powerful inspiration for you. It is a reminder that you have incredible power to actualize your dreams.

WILLIAM KAMKWAMBA

William Kamkwamba is a Malawian inventor and author who rose to fame for his incredible determination and ingenuity in the face of adversity. Born into a poor family in a rural village, Kamkwamba faced numerous challenges throughout his childhood, including poverty, famine, and a lack of access to education.

Despite these challenges, Kamkwamba was passionate about learning and inventing from a young age. He would often scavenge through local junkyards and waste dumps for spare parts and materials to build his own gadgets and machines.

In 2001, a severe drought struck his village, leading to widespread famine and devastation. Unable to afford food or basic necessities, Kamkwamba was forced to drop out of school and spend most of his days tending to the family farm.

While the drought lasted, Kamkwamba was determined to find a solution to the drought and help his community. So, he began to research wind turbines and renewable energy. Using old bicycle parts and scrap metal, he built his own windmill generator, which provided electricity to his family's home and irrigation to their crops.

News of Kamkwamba's invention quickly spread, and he soon became a local celebrity. His story inspired many others in his village to pursue their own dreams and goals, despite their challenging circumstances.

Born To Dream

Today, Kamkwamba is a successful inventor, speaker, and author, with a bestselling book, *The Boy Who Harnessed the Wind*, to his name. He has received numerous awards and accolades for his work in renewable energy and innovation. His story serves as a powerful reminder that dreams do come true if we are willing to work hard, and never give up on our goals, no matter how difficult the journey may seem.

ENOCH ADEJARE ADEBOYE

Enoch Adeboye, also known as "Daddy GO," is a Nigerian pastor and leader of the Redeemed Christian Church of God, one of the fastest-growing Christian denominations in the world. His story is an inspiring one that will encourage you to dream big, have strong faith in God, and work hard to achieve your goals.

Born in 1942 in Ifewara, Nigeria, Enoch Adeboye grew up in a humble family and experienced many hardships and challenges throughout his early years. Despite these obstacles, he remained determined to pursue his passion for education.

Eventually, Enoch was able to enroll in school, and he quickly proved to be an excellent student. He went on to earn a bachelor's degree in Mathematics from the University of Nigeria, Nsukka, and a master's degree in Hydrodynamics from the University of Lagos.

Born To Dream

After completing his education, Enoch started teaching at the University of Lagos, but he felt a calling to do something more significant with his life. In 1973, Enoch had a life-changing encounter with Jesus Christ, and he became a born-again Christian. He started attending the Redeemed Christian Church of God, a small church in Lagos, and soon began to devote his life to serving others and sharing God's message of hope, love, and faith. In 1981, Pastor Adeboye became the General Overseer of the RCCG.

Under Adeboye's leadership, the RCCG has grown into one of the largest and most influential Christian organizations in the world, with millions of members in over 196 countries. He has inspired countless people to pursue their dreams, to believe in themselves, and to trust in God's plan for their lives.

Throughout his life, Enoch Adeboye has faced many challenges and setbacks, but he has always remained steadfast in his faith and committed to his vision. He has never been afraid to take risks, to try new things, or to go against the status quo in pursuit of his dreams.

Today, Enoch Adeboye is considered one of the most respected and admired spiritual leaders in the world, and he continues to inspire people of all ages, races, and backgrounds to dream big and to pursue their passions with courage, determination, and faith in God.

Born To Dream

Summarily, these stories reveal that dreams do come true, and that with resilience, and hard work, we can all fulfill our God-given dreams. So, don't give up yet. Don't rest on yesterday's successes, and don't be daunted by the fears that come with tomorrow. Maximize every opportunity you have today, and lean on God to fulfill the dream He has put in your heart. The world waits for the manifestation of your dreams.

CHAPTER ELEVEN

RELEASE YOURSELF TO LIVE YOUR DREAM

There should be no half-hearted commitment to a vision that God gave you. God does not embrace a half-hearted commitment.

A s young men growing up in suburban African communities, there was this hunting tool we had. We call it catapult. Catapult was a handy, easy-to-use, and simple hunting equipment. From birds to mice, the catapult was our go-to hunting tool. With a stone held between the two elastic strings, the stone can travel a long distance depending on how well you stretched the elastic strings. After stretching the cords, you can then release the stone to go in the direction you desire. If you're good at it, you should no sooner have your kill in your hands.

Like the stone in the stretched catapult, you, too, must release yourself fully into the dream that God gave you – if at all, your dream will see the light of the day. There should be no half-hearted commitment to a vision that God gave you. And God does not embrace a half-hearted commitment. Truth be told, no successful dream arrives at the place of success without receiving a hundred percent devotion of time and resources. So, break free from every fear and uncertainties limiting you, and plunge yourself into the dream that God has given you.

The Biblical Gideon had every reason not to embrace the dream that the angel of the Lord shared with him. He reeled out all the factors that would prevent him from accomplishing the vision.

> *And the LORD turned to him and said, "Go in this might of yours and save Israel from the hand of Midian; do not I send you?" 15 And he said to him, "Please, Lord, how can I save Israel? Behold, my clan is the weakest in Manasseh, and I am the least in my father's house."*

It is true that when God gives us a dream, it is usually larger than our minds can fully comprehend when placed side-by-side with our capacity. But we must trust the God who gave the dream in the first place. When Gideon began to embrace the dream rather than his inabilities, He began to see the capabilities of God.

So, here's the principle: whatever you can see, you can become. If you see your inabilities, you'll remain crippled and unable to carry God's vision for your life. But if you see what God is seeing and His limitless capacity to get your dream fulfilled, you'll become just that and release yourself fully into your dream.

This is what happened in Genesis 30. In the story, Jacob caused the sheep to see the picture of a rod with stripes on them as they mate. The image they saw resulted in the outcome they received. Whatsoever you internalize will ultimately become your outcome. In Proverbs 23:7, the Scripture says

For as he thinketh in his heart, so is he: Eat and drink, saith he to thee; But his heart is not with thee. (KJV)

You do not become your thought; as a matter of fact, that is who you are. What God thought, he spoke, and what he spoke came to be. There is a strong correlation between thinking and being. If you want to change your outcome, change your thinking. With these assertions, you must do all that you can to ensure that only the right information gets to your heart. No wonder the Scripture encourages us to guard our heart in Proverbs 23:4

Keep your heart with all vigilance, for from it flow the springs of life.

I like the way the New Century Version puts it:

Be careful what you think, because your thoughts run your life.

Anything that finds its way into your heart will run your life. If you can see it that way, I am sure you will put in more effort to protect your heart because it determines who you really are. You should be careful about what you hear, watch, read or where you even go to. If it were possible, you will employ external security operatives to protect your heart.

Little wonder, God births a dream in our heart. This is because if the dream can find its way into our heart, then we can become it. Don't neglect that dream in your heart. If it can get there, then God knows that it can come to life. Everything that you need to fulfill your God-given dream is within you. Gideon didn't know this, even when the Lord referred to him as a 'Mighty man of valor.' Therefore, he questioned God, reeling out his resume of weaknesses.

How did I know that everything you need to fulfil your God-given dream is within you?

Genesis 1:11-12 has the answer:

And God said, "Let the earth sprout vegetation, plants yielding seed, and fruit trees bearing fruit in which is their seed, each according to its kind, on the earth." And it was so. 12 The earth brought forth vegetation, plants yielding seed according to their own kinds, and trees bearing fruit in which is their seed, each according to its kind. And God saw that it was good.

God created the plants with their seed in them for multiplication and procreation. So, from the beginning of the world, God had put within the plant the ability to replicate itself. The same is true for us as humans, everything that we need to fulfill our dream is already within us. Though you have everything within you to fulfill your dream, you must believe it to experience it, and more than just believing it, you must take action.

It's like the story of three birds sitting on a wall. Repeatedly, they told themselves they believe they could fly. After about an hour, they kept repeating it to themselves, but they never flew. Your belief is evident by your action. If you believe your dream, you will do everything it takes to pursue it. The evidence of your belief is your action or your pursuit. Your belief must move you to do something about it.

There are people out there that claim they believe God but are never moved into action. In James 2, the writer tells us that the devil believes there is God and trembles. But his actions prove otherwise. So, your belief must always be backed with actions that align with the dream God gave you, for faith without works is dead.

James 2:19-26 says

> *You believe that God is one; you do well. Even the demons believe—and shudder! 20 Do you want to be shown, you foolish person, that faith apart from works is useless? 21 Was not Abraham our father justified by works when he offered up his son Isaac on the altar? 22 You see that faith was active along with his works, and faith was completed by his works; 23 and the*

Scripture was fulfilled that says, "Abraham believed God, and it was counted to him as righteousness"—and he was called a friend of God. 24 You see that a person is justified by works and not by faith alone. 25 And in the same way was not also Rahab the prostitute justified by works when she received the messengers and sent them out by another way? 26 For as the body apart from the spirit is dead, so also faith apart from works is dead.

What you see on the inside of you must move you to act. When David confronted Goliath, he had faith that he could kill Goliath and, therefore, he did not run away. David believed he could kill Goliath by God's help. As a matter of fact, he had pictured God kill Goliath in his mind before the battle began. That was why even before he killed him, he was bold enough to tell him he would cut off his head.

Most of us believe we can kill the Goliath in our lives, but are waiting for the God in us to come out and kill the Goliath for us. We must understand that God has given us all the authority we need to deal with the powers of darkness and make things happen here on earth.

The Scripture says in 1 Samuel 17:45,

Then David said to the Philistine, "You come to me with a sword and with a spear and with a javelin, but I come to you in the name of the LORD of hosts, the God of the armies of Israel, whom you have defied.

David approached Goliath with what he had in his possession – five stones and a sling. You may not have a sling and stones, but that dream in your heart is equally as potent, if only you believe God to use it. In the same manner that David brought out the stones from his purse and used it, you, too, can birth that dream from your heart and pursue it.

I can't overemphasize the need for you to believe your dream enough to pursue it. Maybe you're saying to yourself right now that you do not have anyone to help you out. And that may be true. But the first thing you need is not someone's help but the help of God. And God has helped you by putting the dream in your heart. Now it's your duty to align with this divine help and pursue it. Begin to make up your mind as you read this book to take deliberate steps today about that dream in your heart. You might want to pray about it, speak to someone about it, or do some research about it. Only make sure to take a definitive step today. Ensure you do something deliberate and significant that will set you in motion. Make some intentional movements to accomplish that dream in your heart today, no matter how small you think it may be.

Born To Dream

The devil might come to you with his lies, saying that your efforts will lead nowhere, or that the dream will fail. Don't believe his many lies. Don't give them a chance in your heart. He might also trigger fear in your heart. But remember that God's Word tells us not less than three hundred and sixty-five times to "fear not." The implication is that you have enough of "fear not" to last for each day of the year. Listen to what Pope John Paul XXIII said: "Consult not your fears but your hopes and your dreams. Think not about the frustrations, but about your unfulfilled potential. Concern yourself not with what you tried and failed in, but with what is possible for you to do."

While you overcome the fear of not being able to achieve your dreams, you must also stay away from evil. The context of Judges 6:8-13 reveals that, God hates evil. Each time you do evil, you expose yourself to be afflicted by the devil. You put yourself in a vulnerable position. It is like a cause and effect. The Israelites sinned against God, and they were afflicted by the Midianites.

This reminded me of an incidence that happened during my High School days in Nigeria. We had a teacher who was very mean to the students. Whenever he wanted to punish a student who had erred, he went about it as though he had a score to settle with the student. As this continued, some students thought to get back at the teacher. He had a farm around the students' hostel where he planted maize. The students waited for the corns to bring forth the blades – just about the time for the fruit to form. Then they entered the farm, and uprooted all the maize plants. The sight of this devastated the teacher, but the students had taken their pound of flesh.

When we are on the Lord's side and always dealing with the devil, he looks for an opportunity to get back at us. Such opportunities open up when we sin against God. We expose ourselves to the devil to take advantage of us. That's why 1 John 1:9 says if we sin, Jesus is faithful and just to forgive us and to cleanse us from all unrighteousness. Run to God when you sin and not away from Him.

The Israelites were under the siege of the Midianites, not knowing that God had already made a way of escape for them in Gideon. When God wants to deliver a people, He sends a prophet to them. I want you to know that you are the sent one to your family, that organization or even your country. You are the solution we have been waiting for. Unfortunately, rather than look inward, you look elsewhere for the solution that God has embedded in you.

Look at the mirror right now. The image before you is the solution. In Genesis 45:5 Joseph said,

And now do not be distressed or angry with yourselves because you sold me here, for God sent me before you to preserve life.

Joseph was the solution to his family. He understood that his current position was not just about him, but God bringing him to a place where he could help his family. Look around you, what are you currently enjoying? God brought you there for someone or some people. Please, don't forget that. When the angel spoke with Gideon and told him that he was a mighty man of valor, Gideon, still did not look inwards. Instead, he generalized what the angel told him based on what was also happening in the life of others.

Gideon asked, 'If God was with us, why are we going through all this? Why are miracles that happened in the past no longer happening now (paraphrased)?' You must realize that God deals with us as individuals and we will give an account of what he has called us to do as individuals and not as a community. The solution is already in you. So, look inward.

To the problems of Israel at that time, the Lord provided a solution in Gideon. Gideon was their deliverer. But instead of Gideon delivering the people of Israel, he was using his might for something else, threshing wheat. How tricky can the enemy be! Gideon derived some fulfillment because he was using his might for something that was kind of similar to what he was to do. He was delivering wheat! The enemy will always give an alternative for the real deal. How can a deliverer of Israel be delivering wheat? The deliverer himself was hiding, threshing wheat at the winepress.

Born To Dream

Each time you buy into an alternative idea instead of the real deal, you're invariably hiding. In other words, you can never come to the limelight by engaging in the alternatives for your life. It does not matter the accolades or the fame you get, as long as all you are dealing with is not the real deal, then you are still in hiding. I can imagine people talking about how good he was threshing wheat and giving him great accolades. But he was not fulfilling his purpose yet. When the angel addressed Gideon, he called him by what God had put inside him. He called him a mighty man of valor. I know you think you have not birthed that dream yet, but God is already seeing you as a mother, an entrepreneur, a pilot or whatever dream he has put in your heart.

The good news is that God believes in you. But do you believe in yourself? Definitely, Gideon did not believe in himself, else he would not be in hiding. He had excuses because he felt he was not a mighty man of valor. Yet that did not change the salutation of the angel. A man of valor means a strong man, a mighty man, a courageous man and a valiant man. All these were quite the opposite of what Gideon saw in himself.

When you look at this closely, you will discover that there are many people out there like Gideon, arguing with God about the dream he has put inside them. For us to enjoy the fullness of the dream, we must first of all believe the dream and pursue it. You, like Gideon, might have reasons not to believe the dream. There are many reasons people don't believe their dreams. Let's examine some of the reasons people don't believe the dream that God has put in them.

WHY DON'T WE BELIEVE OUR DREAM?

1. One reason we may not believe our dream is because we extrapolate our dreams from our current situation or position. In other words, we cannot see a direct correlation of where we are with where we are going. How can a prisoner see himself as a prime minister? How can someone who is threshing wheat in hiding at the winepress see himself as a deliverer of his people?

The travails of the Israelites were so great that Gideon could not believe that God was with them. How can God be with you and you are going through so much trouble? Many people, including Christians, believe that a person with many problems must have offended God. Remember the story of Job; his friends also had the same thinking. Job couldn't have been going through all he went through and claim he is righteous. It turned out the issues he went through did not have anything to do with him sinning or not.

It does not take God more might to change a story, no matter how bad it may look. If God created the world in six days, he can change your story in a second. The story was told in 2 Kings 7. Elisha said to the King of Israel,

But Elisha said, "Hear the word of the LORD: thus says the LORD, Tomorrow about this time a seah of fine flour shall be sold for a shekel, and two seahs of barley for a shekel, at the gate of Samaria." 2 Then the captain on whose hand the king leaned said to the man of God, "If the LORD himself should make windows in heaven, could this thing be?" 2 Kings 78:1-2

The man of God replied him and said:

"You shall see it with your own eyes, but you shall not eat of it."

Everything happened just as the man of God said. Four lepers went to the camp of the Syrians and discovered that they had run away because of the noise they heard. They came back to the king and told him what they saw and lo and behold, the words of the man of God came to pass. Our God works in mysterious ways and can change your story overnight.

2. Another reason we do not believe our dreams is because of the battles we are going through in our lives. This is closely related to the first reason. We are simply unable to see how God can manifest that dream based on what is happening around us. Additionally, we cannot see the manifestation of the dream because we also hold the belief that 'If God is with us, we will not be going through what we are going through.'

Born To Dream

This was one of the reasons Gideon gave. The Israelites were being oppressed by the Midianites. How can I be impoverished by an enemy nation and still say that God is with me? In several instances, when we see a great opposition, we tend to think that God is not with us. We tend to forget that the opposition may be because the devil sees a great destiny ahead of us. Joseph went from the pit to Potiphar's house, then to the prison before going to the palace. As a matter of fact, when he was a slave in Potiphar's house, it was written about him that God was with him (Genesis 39:2). You must never let the situation you find yourself define you.

Our God can never be reduced to an experience. God is always bigger than any experience you've had, may be having or will ever have. The scripture says that let all men be liars and let God alone be true (Romans 3:4). That situation is part of the lies from the devil regarding the capabilities and love of God towards you. Our God is capable of taking you from the prison to the palace in one second or from the backside of the desert to the palace. If someone had told Mephibosheth that he would, one day, seat and dine with the king he would not have believed it. He would have said, 'Me, a cripple. How can that be?' But God is not a man. He works in mysterious ways. Don't relate with a man based on what he is going through at the moment. He might be down today but he will not be down forever.

Born To Dream

Our God is bigger than any experience or predicament that a man could be going through.

3. When you expect help but it's not coming, you might want to disbelieve your dream. This happens when you look to others to come to your aid in fulfilling your dream. In other words, when help is not in sight, you believe the dream is not from God. When the angel met Gideon and told him he was a mighty man of valor, Gideon began talking about things happening in the community. He could not see his dream fulfilled because he felt the fulfillment of his dream was a collective affair – everyone was impoverished.

Your dream is not a collective affair. It is a personal affair. In spite of the things happening or not happening around you, learn to look inwards. The Lord had promised Caleb that he was going to give him a mountain. But Caleb, even at the age of 85, still held on to the word of God and requested for the mountain (Josh 14:12-15). Caleb was not content seeing that the lands were being shared to the children of Israel. He held on to what God told him even when age was against him, and requested for what he knew was his from heaven. This implies that Caleb carried that dream in his heart for 45 years. As long as he was alive, He was persuaded that God would fulfill his word.

4. Another reason Christians do not believe their dream is that they do not believe they have any supernatural ability. You must realize that you are not ordinary. As one who has been born-again, you are born of God (1 John 5:4). Therefore, you are born an overcomer. Our God is a supernatural being. If God gave birth to you then you are also a supernatural being and therefore, have the DNA of God. Our God dreams and that's how He created the world. You also have the dreaming genes and that's how you will also create your own world. Don't be deceived, you are a spirit, you have a soul and live in a body. You are supernatural and those things you see on your inside, you should birth on the outside just like God did.

As we continue, I want to highlight certain things about dreams that will enable you believe and live the dream that God has put in your heart.

HOW DO I BELIEVE MY DREAM?

1. The fulfillment of your dream is based on the Integrity of God

Hebrews 10:23 says

Let us hold fast the confession of our hope without wavering, for he who promised is faithful.

Hebrews 6:13-18 says,

For when God made a promise to Abraham, since he had no one greater by whom to swear, he swore by himself, 14 saying, "Surely I will bless you and multiply you." 15 And thus Abraham, having patiently waited, obtained the promise. 16 For people swear by something greater than themselves, and in all their disputes an oath is final for confirmation. 17 So when God desired to show more convincingly to the heirs of the promise the unchangeable character of his purpose, he guaranteed it with an oath, 18 so that by two unchangeable things, in which it is impossible for God to lie, we who have fled for refuge might have strong encouragement to hold fast to the hope set before us.

Our God is a God of integrity. He does whatever He says and He says whatever He does. When God shows you a dream, it is because he intends to fulfill it. You can be sure that God will always play His own part of the deal. But will you fulfill your own part of the deal? A dream from God does not entirely rest on Him to be fulfilled; we also need to know that we have to believe it and run with it.

2. **Based on the ability of God**

Hebrews 11:11 says,

By faith Sarah herself received power to conceive, even when she was past the age, since she considered him faithful who had promised.

1 Sam 17:34-37 also says this:

But David said to Saul, "Your servant used to keep sheep for his father. And when there came a lion, or a bear, and took a lamb from the flock, 35 I went after him and struck him and delivered it out of his mouth. And if he arose against me, I caught him by his beard and struck him and killed him. 36 Your servant has struck down both lions and bears, and this uncircumcised Philistine shall be like one of them, for he has defied the armies of the living God." 37 And David said, "The LORD who delivered me from the paw of the lion and from the paw of the bear will deliver me from the hand of this Philistine." And Saul said to David, "Go, and the LORD be with you!"

The Bible says in Daniel 3:17,

If this be so, our God whom we serve is able to deliver us from the burning fiery furnace, and he will deliver us out of your hand, O king.

One reason I like this God is that He is able. His ability cannot be questioned. We live in a time when people have all sorts of gods that cannot save them. Remember the story of Dagon in 1 Samuel 5. When the Ark of the Covenant went into the house of Dagon, it kept falling headlong like humpty dumpty. Dagon was a powerless god, an impotent god that lacked ability.

3. **Based on your belief and your words**

Born To Dream

Paul wrote in Romans 10:8:

> *But what does it say? "The word is near you, in your mouth and in your heart" (that is, the word of faith that we proclaim); 9 because, if you confess with your mouth that Jesus is Lord and believe in your heart that God raised him from the dead, you will be saved. 10 For with the heart one believes and is justified, and with the mouth one confesses and is saved.*

Born To Dream

Mark 9 23 says

And Jesus said to him, "'If you can'! All things are possible for one who believes."

The Scripture also says in Hebrews 3:18-4:1

And to whom did he swear that they would not enter his rest, but to those who were disobedient? 19 So we see that they were unable to enter because of unbelief. 1 Therefore, while the promise of entering his rest still stands, let us fear lest any of you should seem to have failed to reach it.

Hebrews 4:2 declares that

For good news came to us just as to them, but the message they heard did not benefit them, because they were not united by faith with those who listened.

You must believe your dream. Your belief is so powerful, that no matter how big or lofty that dream is, without you believing it, it will never come to pass. You may say God can do all things and you are correct. But He needs you to believe your dream. The evidence of your belief is what we hear from your mouth. You must confess what you believe. The world is yours for the taking. And God is with you every step of the journey to help you realize the dreams He kept in your heart.

REFERENCES

"Anand Kumar Super 30 Story, Biography, Success Story, Admission -..." My Site, www.mbarendezvous.com/motivational-story/anand-kumar/. Accessed 1 June 2023.

Carson, Ben. Gifted Hands. Zondervan, 9 Sept. 2008.

Conot, Robert E, and Matthew Josephson. "Thomas Edison | Biography, Inventions, & Facts." Encyclopedia Britannica, 26 Oct. 2018, www.britannica.com/biography/Thomas-Edison.

Enoch: The biopic on the life of Adejare Adeboye. Directed by John Oguntuase and Damilola Mike-Bamiloye, Solid Rock Foundation and Mount Zion Film Productions, 2023.

Hidden Figures. Directed by Theodore Melfi, 20th Century Fox, 10 Dec. 2016.

"Hidden No More: Black Women Groundbreakers at NASA." Si.edu, 2 Nov. 2021, airandspace.si.edu/stories/editorial/hidden-no-more-black-women-groundbreakers-nasa.

Hochfelder, David. "Alexander Graham Bell | Biography, Inventions, & Facts." Encyclopedia Britannica, 30 Nov. 2018, www.britannica.com/biography/Alexander-Graham-Bell.

Kaku, Michio. "Albert Einstein | Biography, Education, Discoveries, & Facts." Encyclopedia Britannica, 20 Sept. 2018, www.britannica.com/biography/Albert-Einstein.

Library of Congress. "Life of Thomas Alva Edison | Biography | Articles and Essays | Inventing Entertainment: The Early Motion

Pictures and Sound Recordings of the Edison Companies | Digital Collections | Library of Congress." The Library of Congress, 2015,

Paranick, Amber. ""Behind Asylum Bars:" Nellie Bly Reporting from Blackwell's Island. | Headlines and Heroes." Blogs.loc.gov, 8 Nov. 2022, blogs.loc.gov/headlinesandheroes/2022/11/nellie-bly-blackwells-island/.

Something the Lord Made. Directed by Joseph Sargent, HBO Films, 30 May 2004.

Super 30. Directed by Vikas Bahl, Reliance Entertainment and PVR Pictures, 12 July 2019.

The Boy Who Harnessed the Wind. Directed by Chiwetel Ejiofor, Netflix, 15 Jan. 2019.

The Editors of Encyclopedia Britannica. "Nellie Bly | American Journalist." Encyclopædia Britannica, 23 Jan. 2019, www.britannica.com/biography/Nellie-Bly.

The New Man. "Biography of Pastor Enoch Adejare Adeboye." The New Man, 21 May 2023, www.thenewman.org.ng/2020/05/biography-of-pastor-eadeboye.html. Accessed 1 June 2023.

"Vivien Thomas · the Blue Baby Operation · Exhibits: The Sheridan Libraries and Museums." Exhibits.library.jhu.edu, exhibits.library.jhu.edu/exhibits/show/the-blue-baby-operation/vivien-thomas.

Vujicic, Nick. "Nick Biography – Life without Limbs." Lifewithoutlimbs.org, lifewithoutlimbs.org/about/nick-biography/.

Vujicic, Nick. Life without Limits: Inspiration for a Ridiculously Good Life. Colorado Springs, Colorado, Waterbrook Press, 2012.

www.loc.gov/collections/edison-company-motion-pictures-and-sound-recordings/articles-and-essays/biography/life-of-thomas-alva-edison/.

ABOUT THE BOOK

Born to Dream: This captivating book delves deep into the essence of dreaming and igniting the fire within your soul.

Who is a dreamer? Why do we dream? Dr. John Itakpe fearlessly tackles these profound questions, inviting you on a transformative journey of self-discovery and empowerment. With unwavering hope and practical guidance, Born to Dream becomes a beacon of light in your pursuit of resilience, calling you to seize every opportunity that comes your way.

Through the pages of this book, Dr. Itakpe's powerful message resounds: lean on the wisdom of God, trust in divine timing, and fearlessly chase after the dreams woven into the very fabric of your being. It's a clarion call to realize your life's purpose, a purpose that brings joy to both God and humanity while leaving an indelible impact on the world.

Prepare to be captivated as Dr. Itakpe shares profound insights, empowering you to live a life brimming with purpose, passion, and unwavering faith. Within these sacred words, you'll discover the keys to unlocking your full potential, as you boldly leave your unique mark upon the tapestry of existence.

Born To Dream

Dive into the wisdom held within these pages and embrace the transformative power of dreaming, for within you lies the seed of greatness. The world eagerly awaits the manifestation of your dreams. Let Born to Dream be your guide on this remarkable journey of self-discovery and fulfillment.

ABOUT THE AUTHOR

Dr. John Itakpe, a dynamic and sought-after minister whose impact on the community is nothing short of remarkable. As the lead pastor of Mercy Court, an energetic parish of the Redeemed Christian Church of God, he is lovingly referred to as PJ by his devoted congregation.

Driven by an unwavering passion for teaching God's word and a profound love for Him, Dr. Itakpe envisions a world where individuals embody the character of Christ and utilize their unique God-given gifts to effect positive change. He firmly believes that encountering God opens the door to a life overflowing with abundant joy and fulfillment.

Beyond his spiritual guidance, his expertise extends to the realm of research science, where he commands respect as a distinguished professional in a prestigious pharmaceutical company located in Bethesda, Maryland. Prior to his successful career in research, he dedicated over a decade to dentistry, showcasing his unwavering commitment to service.

Dr. Itakpe's thirst for knowledge led him to the United States, where he achieved a Master of Public Health from the renowned Johns Hopkins Bloomberg School of Public Health. This academic journey culminated in the attainment of a Doctor of Public Health degree from Morgan State University, Maryland, USA.

In his personal life, Dr. Itakpe finds immense joy and inspiration in his cherished union with his beloved wife, Rosemary. Together, they are blessed with three remarkable daughters who bring boundless happiness to their family. Residing in the captivating city of Ellicott City, Maryland, they embrace a life centered on faith and purpose.

Prepare to embark on a captivating journey filled with Dr. John Itakpe's extraordinary experiences and profound insights. Brace yourself for inspiration as he invites you to embrace a life empowered by unwavering faith and unwavering purpose.

Connect With Me On Social Media

Instagram: https://www.Instagram.com/johnitakpe

Facebook: https://www.Facebook.com/itakpe.john

LinkedIn: https://www.linkedin.com/in/john-itakpe-62aa2519

Born To Dream

Forward all your messages and inquires to: **Email Address**:

johnitakpe@gmail.com